I'm
ONLY
HERE
for the
WiFi

Books published by Running Press are available at special discounts
for bulk purchases in the United States by corporations, institutions,
and other organizations. For more information, please contact the Special
Markets Department at the Perseus Books Group, 2300 Chestnut Street,
Suite 200, Philadelphia, PA 19103, or call (800) 810-4145, ext. 5000,
or e-mail special.markets@perseusbooks.com.

ISBN 978-0-7624-4913-2
Library of Congress Control Number: 2013934595

E-book ISBN 978-0-7624-5062-6

9   8   7   6   5   4   3   2   1
Digit on the right indicates the number of this printing

Cover and interior design by Amanda Richmond
Edited by Jordana Tusman
Typography: Governor, Gotham, and Archer

Running Press Book Publishers
2300 Chestnut Street
Philadelphia, PA 19103-4371

Visit us on the web!
www.runningpress.com

I'm ONLY HERE for the WiFi

A COMPLETE GUIDE TO RELUCTANT ADULTHOOD

CHELSEA FAGAN

RUNNING PRESS
PHILADELPHIA · LONDON

To Isabella,

for whenever you think you want to give up.
Just remember: Legal alcohol is right around the
corner, and it exceeds your wildest dreams.

CONTENTS

INTRODUCTION

Walk into a coffee shop this Wednesday afternoon. What would you expect to see? After all, it's the time of the week when most people should be attending to whatever activity they've chosen to contribute to society—leisure time, as we were raised to understand it, is usually relegated to evenings and weekends. And yet, as if the whole world has just stopped turning and the laws of economics have ceased to apply, the coffee shop will be filled with young, able-bodied humans. Physically adept, intellectually curious, they have all coalesced to nibble on the same stale muffin for four hours and do all but build a makeshift shelter at the back table by the bathroom. With almost no regard to the idea that WiFi, as well as table space itself, costs money, the entire entity of a coffee shop has been usurped by people determined to linger over the same cup of drip coffee for an entire afternoon. Tapping away on $1,500 computers, you'll see a whole branch of society hard at work doing, well, whatever it is they do.

And what is that, exactly? It could be any number of things. Sure, there will be the vacant horde who have long since given up on their dreams and have resigned themselves to aimless Facebook cruising. There will be the networkers, updating their Twitter and LinkedIn profiles (just kidding—LinkedIn is for people who have to go to offices), making those powerful social connections. There will be freelancers, whose incomes range from "whatever my parents put on the card this month" to "secret billionaire," but those are deceptively hard to spot in a crowd. What is sure, though, is that this is where they are safe. This is where they won't be judged, save for the occasional hateful glance from the guy picking up the empty cups and resenting the fact that somehow he got stuck having to work an actual job.

We've all read endless articles and studies about how monumentally directionless our young people are, in everything from *The New York Times* to *Slate*, and while it's so easy to turn up your nose and tell us to indiscriminately "get a life," it's not hard to see why the situation is so bleak. Since we were old enough to know the sweet, sweet ecstasy of a gold star on a sheet of paper, we've been told to go to college. We've been told to dream big, because there is nothing we couldn't do. We've been told to pursue any- and everything, from ballerina to astronaut to teacher to doctor, and promised that with enough vigor and tuition, we'd achieve it. Several years and trillions of dollars of student debt later, we've realized that it's just not like that. We've moved grudgingly back into our parents' basements, or in hopeful flocks toward the Great Cities on the hill—Portland, New York, Philly, D.C., L.A.—to continue to pursue a dream, only this time with well over $1,000-a-month rents and jobs we always haughtily imagined would be beneath us at twenty-three. Reality is repeatedly splashing us in the face with ever-colder water, and our preconceived notions about everything have turned out to be, at best, wrong, and, at worst, incredibly expensive.

Those of us who moved to cities, though, have the added bonus of being surrounded by those who did "make it" in whatever sense we've long imagined that to be. Somehow affording an extravagant wedding at twenty-five, working a respectable position at a high-powered PR firm (who even believed those still existed?), or living in an apartment that seems too well-decorated to belong to someone who still does beer bongs—these are all proof that it's possible. We come across people who walk around with all this "money" we've heard so much about, with places to go and a reason to look down on those who've been left behind. You don't know the true existential cruelty of the social hierarchy until you've been forced to go to a brunch with twenty-two-year-olds who make $55K a year doing something they love. People who, a few mere months ago, may have been your close friends, now see you as something to be pitied, to be studied—a cautionary tale. "Oh, what are you doing? That sounds ... fun." No, it doesn't. Working days at the Gap and nights babysitting does not sound fun to anyone, and your condescending lies aren't canceling out your Marc Jacobs purse. We get it: Some people are more successful than others, and now, more than ever, that makes the special ones even more special.

Navigating just a single day as a young urban human being—whether professional or whatever the politically correct antithesis of that is—is an exercise in adaptation. We've learned to be entitled, to be fragile, and, yet, to be hopeful. All these things, in varying measure, prove to be in need of an extremely large grain of salt. Sure, great things can happen, but they likely take time. Yes, you should want success, but you may want to be flexible on the definition. Sure, emotions are necessary, but they cannot dictate your entire life. And if we don't learn to accept these truths and adjust our lives accordingly, we could end up like so many of our fallen comrades, spending days on end at the coffee shop, inciting the ire of every barista to ever glare at us over the pastry case.

But from waking up in the morning, to slogging through public transportation (in all its urine-soaked forms), to putting in hours wherever we've chosen to put them, all the way down to deciding between a yardstick of shots with someone you just met waiting in line for the bathroom or going to bed at 9:00 p.m. like an adult—it's all so much. We were promised that life was going to be riding around on a unicorn in a business suit, collecting gold coins, and moving into apartments that are less and less dependent on IKEA. We were promised the world.

It seems as though everyone lied to us. If you watched *Sex and the City*, you imagined that even if you look like Sarah Jessica Parker and have a personality akin to taking a cheese grater to the back of the calves, men will still fawn all over you. You will have your pick of the litter, and can go through dates, suitors, and engagements like a carousel that you only step off once every week or so to get drunk and go on a shopping spree with girl-friends. If you listened to college brochures and advisors, you imagined a long line of men and women in business suits waiting for you outside of college graduation wearing a name tag that says *boss*, and gleefully handing you a contract where you get paid $50K a year to gchat and have three-martini lunch meetings. If you listened to well-meaning relatives, you imagined that owning a house and settling down by the age of twenty-seven was not only what was expected, it was also going to be that magical line of painter's tape across your life that designated the shift from "child" to "adult." I think we can safely say that none of these things are realistic, and most are dangerous to believe in. To not feel like a disappointment in at least one category is to either be kidding yourself or to be too insufferable and perfect to even speak to. For your sake, I hope it's the former.

Yet, every day is a new chapter, the journey of a thousand miles begins with a single step, and other clichés. I firmly believe that if we can just make it through this day, and the next, something is bound to pop up. Maybe just take yourself less seriously, accept that your mom may not be gloating about your job at whatever boring mom meet-up groups she goes to, and learn to laugh a tiny bit at the overall bleakness of the situation. I know that we'll likely be reading endless articles over the next ten years about how the dating prospects are bad, the job prospects are LOL, and the real estate market is essentially breaking our collective kneecaps, but it's really not so bad. You'll see—deep down, we're all in this together. Yes, even that girl on the subway every morning with the manicure, dry-cleaned skirt suit, energy smoothie, and not a hair out of place—she's in it, too. She's struggling to figure it out somehow. And if she's not, well, we'll push her off a cliff. I promise.

For now, though, we'll all find a warm spot to congregate while we bemoan our respective difficulties in finding our place on the socioeconomic ladder. For some, it will be in the break room of a terrible temp job. For others, it will be at a house party on a Friday night where no one judges you for bringing a bottle of Boone's or Mad Dog because everyone is broke. For still others, it will be at a coffee shop. It may not be the proudest moment of our lives, but at least we know that we'll be able to work on our computers until the manager starts shooting us dirty looks around shift-change time. This is the land of milk and honey: The caffeine is hot, the Muzak is inoffensive, and the WiFi is unlimited. This is home.

Chapter 1

THE MORNING

Or, How Hard You Can
Throw the Alarm Clock
Before It Will Break

I should probably say, right off the bat, that I am not a morning person. I know that such people exist, and I know that they are the ones largely running society, inventing new technologies, and ridding the world of disease. I know that they are a necessary—if not *the* most necessary—part of society. But I, quite simply, am not one of them. I often wonder how much easier, healthier, and more lucrative my life would be if I were one of those people who jumps out of bed at 7:00 a.m. and butterfly kisses her motivational poster (as I imagine all morning people do), but I doubt I'll ever reach such a lofty status. For me, and I assume for many of you, mornings will always be a bit of a struggle.

So things are already off to a bad start, reaching over and slapping the alarm clock. Depending on where you are in your twenties—and in your life—there could be any number of things you're off to do. School, for those who are prolonging it painfully throughout as many years as they possibly can, perpetually deferring adulthood and paying off loans by accruing more loans (I assume in hopes of marrying a Saudi oil tycoon the day of their graduation with a master's in creative writing). Work, for those who have either been lucky enough to get a "real" job or are slogging through with one that pays the bills and funds brunch two weekends a month. And then, for some of us, setting an alarm and giving us a time of day (arbitrary as it may be) to get up and join humanity is just a small, innocuous way to keep some kind of sanity, since being unemployed and living in your parents' basement can become a slippery slope into delusion without a little routine.

Mornings, in any case, are full of checklists. Whether or not we write them down (and if you are the kind of person capable of physically making checklists and actually moving through them with some kind of accuracy, you will never know how I envy you), it is essential that we have at least some kind of routine. Some step-by-step process that we can hone and master as we grow up and begin to see life as not just one large obstacle, but a series of smaller, more refined obstacles that can be traversed if taken in small enough increments. And with any day's tasks ahead of us, it is essential that we start things off on the right foot with our mental checklists, though it would be a lie to pretend that some things are harder to wake up for than others.

Perhaps the most unsatisfying of all the possible reasons to be waking up is for the menial work that many of us are forced to take to pay the bills, the kind of job that provides the Triple Crown of young adult despair and:

· Calls for long, tedious hours of barely compensated work that requires only a high school diploma (if that) to attain, and is filled with people we secretly despise/feel superior to on some sick level. Usually comes with a manager who is everything we want to avoid when we are his age.

· Has absolutely no value in terms of telling your parents; their horrendous, judgmental friends; or your own friends who have known the sweet taste of professional success.

- Leaves you perpetually in the hellish limbo of needing the job for the bare necessities it provides you with, and, despite your lack of respect for the position or your coworkers, finds you utterly disposable and replaceable.

Now, don't get me wrong: Not every service, retail, or temp job is going to be such a soul drain, but it certainly makes getting up every day feel all the less satisfying. It promotes that ritualistic early-morning conversation with yourself, the one in which you debate quitting the stupid job because you could probably spread your cash super-thin and make it through the time it would take to find another job scooping ice cream or doing something like that. As the economy falters, this monologue becomes ever more a farce.

Sure, we've all had moments where we didn't show up or we quit on the spot because we were so fed up with being tethered to a job for which there was zero respect on either side, but how long into "adulthood"—and financial responsibility—is that really going to be an option? There is a vast difference between an impassioned walk-out of your job at Target when you're a carefree eighteen-year-old, and when you're a twenty-five-year-old with evening master's classes and a one-bedroom apartment to pay for.

So the morning routine. What is it supposed to be? What have we always imagined how "adults" transform themselves from a snoring pile of sweatpants into something that could theoretically interact with other humans? Well, at least in my imagination, it has consisted of:

- Set an alarm for a reasonable hour, allowing yourself at most one slap of the snooze button and giving you a perfect window of time to accomplish all that needs to be done before you begin your day.

- Turn off your alarm, get up, stretch, and make your bed behind you.

- Go to your bathroom, and take a relaxing fifteen-minute shower that gives you ample time to both cleanse and have the kind of soul-shattering philosophical epiphanies that only occur while standing naked under hot water.

- Dry and style your hair, apply your flattering but subtle makeup, and go back to your room (not before putting away the things you took out to get ready, of course).

- Stand pensively in front of your closet for approximately 1.23 minutes as you contemplate which outfit would give you the most effective combination of approachability, professionalism, and youthfulness to make the most out of every interaction you will have that day.

- After putting on said outfit, return towels to a drying rack so as not to leave them crumpled and moist on some unsuspecting bedroom furniture.

- Go to the bar in your kitchen (because you are an adult, and your kitchen has a bar on which to eat your less formal meals).

- Spread out for yourself a low-fat Greek yogurt, granola that you made yourself in your oven like a living Etsy doll, some sliced-up fruit (bonus points if it's some crazy-ass Indonesian fruit that no one's ever heard of), and a cup of tea or free-trade coffee with soy milk.

- Eat delicately while you read something for cultured, refined enjoyment, like *The New Yorker, W Magazine, Newsweek, I'm a Pretentious Fop*, or *This Sweater Is Vintage Monthly*.

- Clean and put away all your breakfast accoutrements.

- Get on your adorable bicycle (it's always perfect bike-riding weather, and your bicycle has a basket in which to store work shoes/purses/necessities) and ride off into the fresh morning air.

Now, believe it or not, this has never managed to be how I get ready in the morning. Even on the nights where I chamomile myself into a sleep coma at 8:00 p.m. and psych myself up to the nth degree about how adult my morning is going to be the next day, I will inevitably live out the *Groundhog Day*-esque torture that is my perpetually infantile morning routine:

- Set an alarm for far enough in advance from my actual wake-up time that I can get some decent snooze action and still have wiggle room.

- Hit the snooze no less than six times, waking up only when I look at the clock and let out a muffled "Ohshitjesuschrist!" as I flop out of bed like a dying fish. Leave bed looking like it has been freshly napalmed.

- Take the world's fastest, least efficient shower, not even fully rinsing off the soap before I stumble out and stand in front of the mirror.

- Shake the maximum amount of water out of my hair before putting it into the least aesthetically assaulting style, slap on some makeup (ten gold coins if you can apply liquid eyeliner—the Rubik's Cube of modern cosmetics—without looking like a velvet-painted sad clown), and run back into my bedroom.

- Grab the first outfit that is clean, reasonably color-coordinated, and ironed enough not to look like crumpled-up aluminum foil and throw it on.

- Pick up something from the kitchen as I run out the door to grab some form of public transportation (it's been a while since I've lived in a city that has an even vaguely reasonable ROI on owning a car).

- Find out that I managed to grab a Swiss Cake Roll and an ankle sock in my blind, early-morning haste. Grudgingly eat the Swiss Cake Roll as I avoid the stare of fellow commuters.

Taking time to make mornings a pleasant, refreshing, fulfilling experience just seems impossible. The early twenties is that

THE THINGS WE'RE LIKELY TO DITCH WHEN PRESSED FOR TIME

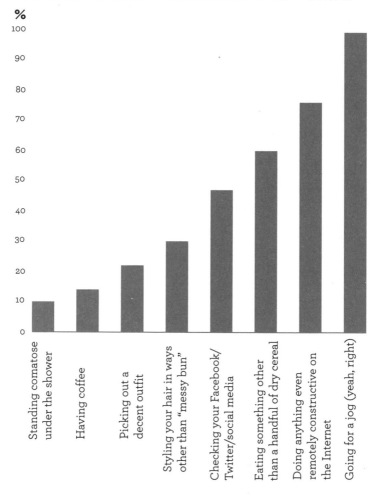

%

100
90
80
70
60
50
40
30
20
10
0

Standing comatose under the shower

Having coffee

Picking out a decent outfit

Styling your hair in ways other than "messy bun"

Checking your Facebook/Twitter/social media

Eating something other than a handful of dry cereal

Doing anything even remotely constructive on the Internet

Going for a jog (yeah, right)

strange limbo where your body—and your douchebag friends—are all insisting you stay out every night to enjoy all the wonders and mysteries your city has to offer (usually costing around $10 a glass), and your body somehow does not have the resilience of a rubber band when it comes to snapping awake in the morning.

And even if I were a morning person, there are so many steps involved, it seems just exhausting. Just eating a balanced breakfast has a myriad components—and people who take Instagram photos of their morning spread cannot honestly be rushing off directly afterward to some soul-crushing job. Who sits there, iPhone in hand, and thinks, "I want to make my entire Twitter community feel inadequate this morning. Look, you peasants. I'm eating sliced kiwi and yogurt with lychee syrup. Don't know what lychee is? I thought you wouldn't't."

So it seems as though three clear obstacles stand in the way of what could be considered an "adult" morning, provided you're able to get up at a reasonable hour. Obviously, setting your alarm and adhering to it is the point upon which your entire day hinges, but there are only so many ways to go about that. Short of hiring someone to hide in your closet until she jumps out at 7:30 and splashes ice water on your face, I'm pretty sure that's just going to be a battle you fight with yourself. You either learn to get up or you don't. But once you've mastered that, there remain clear steps to bring yourself into "full-grown status," and none of them can be left unchecked.

Making Yourself Look Like
an Acceptable Member of Society

I'm not here to lecture you on what fashion is—frankly, I'm the last person who should be talking about that. I see photos from New York Fashion Week and am thoroughly convinced they were taken straight out of *The Onion*. I have no idea what fashion is supposed to look like. (And 99 percent of what I see on The Sartorialist makes me sad for humanity.) But I do know what it means to be presentable, and to at least put together an outfit that will transfer well from work to shopping to socializing in some form or another. Simply presenting yourself like someone who knows vaguely what you're doing seems to be the key to happiness in life, since people are incredibly judgmental and will make assessments about you everywhere from the produce aisle to your job interview. So hedge your bets and put your best foot forward.

But it's often difficult to find that healthy middle ground between "stylish" and "practical" when the kinds of fashion we are told to emulate, as in said fashion shows and street photography blogs, are simply impossible to achieve in real life. Unless you literally ooze money, you are not going to be able to afford nearly anything in most magazines on a regular basis, and people dictating the latest in fashion are rarely eager to explain how to make an on-sale Gap sweater work for you. Finding a way to dress that is both professional and still appropriate for a twentysomething—without selling your kidneys on the black market—is kind of a tricky problem.

So what are we supposed to look like? Skirt suits with bright-colored shirts? Knee-length skirts that our grandmothers would approve of? Day-to-night wrap dresses that forgive nearly any tummy pooch? The kind of liquid eyeliner that somehow makes your eyes just look naturally sexy without screaming, *"Look at the spackle all over my face!"* Sure, these are all probably good calls. And, if you're lucky, your job allows a Zooey Deschanel-esque dress code for women and you can just wear any dress to ever appear on ModCloth. Eventually, getting ready should become, if anything, more an essential list of things to get rid of, and never look back on.

Some things we must leave behind forever:

- **Uggs:** Your feet looking like melting marshmallows stopped being cute years ago.

- **Black leggings:** I don't care if you only wear these to the gym; they are eventually going to work their way into your wardrobe in some actual clothinglike capacity, and before you know it, you're going to be tricking yourself into thinking these are pants. Eventually, you're just going to go out in some body paint and a T-shirt that says *2 Hot 2 Handle*.

- **Anything unsustainably trendy:** Let's put it this way. If you are twenty-six and continue to invest heavily in things like jeggings or endless cardigans with those stupid elbow patches, you deserve to lose all your money to Forever 21.

- **Flip-flops:** Some people like these things, but they are truly the Chicken McNuggets of dressing yourself. They are lazy, unattractive, and, unless accompanied by a pristine pedicure, rather unpleasant to look at. To be reserved for the beach only.

- **Boob curtains:** I am referring here to the dresses and shirts that simply hit you at the boobs and go straight down from there, also known as tent dresses. I don't know why anyone would ever want something that makes her look nine months pregnant when she actually has rock-solid abs, but these continue to be manufactured, so go figure.

- **Butterfly clips:** No explanation needed.

I think it's safe to say that the removal of items like this—and anything else that lives in squalor in the back of your closet, never to be worn again but always to be kept out of some misplaced sense of nostalgia—will ensure at least a decent wardrobe. Because, really, most people look pretty okay, provided they remember to wipe the toothpaste off their shirt and zip their flies up. It's more a question of preventing yourself from ever going for a windbreaker, tennis shoes, sweatpants, or anything of the like when you're running late and temporarily forget that the omniscient eye of society never, ever takes a break.

Eating the Kind of Breakfast
Your Mother Would Approve of

Perhaps I am the only one to have fallen prey to this phenomenon, but I was denied much of any autonomy when it came to my breakfasts as a child. While, yes, looking back, making me eat oatmeal and orange juice and whole wheat toast was probably for the better in terms of my physical and mental development, as a child, I dreamed of breaking free and essentially freebasing spoon after spoon of Fruity Pebbles. I craved sugar, I craved fat, I craved a glass of chocolate milk so deeply brown it was like staring into George Clooney's eyes as he proposed to you. I shouldn't have been left to my own devices, and I wasn't. Thank you, Mom and Dad.

But now that the era of being told what and when to eat is over, and I am essentially set free in a grocery store with a debit card and no idea what trans fat actually is, things are kind of bleak. When I want to reach for a pint of Häagen-Dazs that I know very well I will finish myself, no matter what my original intention, I have no one to stop me. When I have something of an existential crisis in the snack aisle deciding whether Cooler Ranch or Nacho Cheesier better describes me as a person, my mom can't redirect me to the bone-dry pretzel rods. I can unironically buy Cheez Whiz. And never is this complete lack of discretion more apparent than in the things I choose to get for myself in the mornings.

First and foremost, sugary cereals are literally the devil. Even if you buy them with the intent of eating one reasonable bowl every other day with soy or skim milk as a little treat for when you wake up extra early, it will never turn out that way. Ever. Cereal can be eaten (and thoroughly enjoyed) at any time of the day, and in any physical state. Whether in the bowl with milk, crushed up over ice cream, or eaten straight out of the box with impunity, it's always an appropriate time for Reese's Puffs. (Sidenote: What Machiavellian prince sicced such a cereal on the human population? Wasn't life hard enough to keep in balance before we had access to Reese's Cups in powdery ball form?) Anyway, whether it's cereal with the nutritional value of melted plastic, or a stack of pancakes that stares at me with the never-closing eye of Sauron, I can't take care of myself when it comes to morning nourishment.

I have found that the best way to prevent myself from eating such things is simply not to keep them in my kitchen, as I am far too lazy to get up and run to the grocery store at 7:30 in the morning simply to replace my empty Toaster Strudel stock. Normally, this works wonders in keeping me drinking vanilla soy milk and eating bland banana after bland banana. I usually do pretty well. However, this empty-kitchen trap can occasionally lead, in those desperate-for-a-sugary-embrace moments, to a shame-filled trip to that Mecca of twentysomething wastefulness—Starbucks.

Nothing at Starbucks is healthy. Nothing. Even if you get an espresso, judging by its vaguely burnt-rubber aftertaste, I'm assuming you are drinking more straight carcinogens than any-thing else. And, yes, Starbucks's drinks are delicious. We all know that health consciousness is not what drives us there, no matter how much they want to somehow pair up with yoga and "ethnic jazz." Starbucks is not good for your soul. Yet somehow we've man-aged to convince ourselves—especially during those particularly difficult mornings—that drinking twenty ounces of hot milk with a couple squirts of sugar and coffee in it is some kind of breakfast. It is truly the nutritional equivalent of taking your brain out on a nice dinner date only to never call it again. By 11:30, you find your-self staring blankly ahead of you as you are somehow hungry, tired, twitchy, and depressed all at once. Starbucks drinks leave you with this lingering feeling of vague melancholy, only to be swatted away with another $5 spent on twenty minutes of coffee. It's a cycle we should do our best to avoid.

But, like sheep to the slaughter, we'll keep going back. I love Starbucks. I am legally required to, as a twenty-three-year-old urban white woman, but I would like it even if I weren't. It's like getting a lollipop when you were at the bank as a kid, a little bright spot in an otherwise bland day. But this doesn't mean we should become one of those people who are never seen without their sig-nature white cup. The more we can keep the foods like this—as well as the tiny demons like sugary breakfast cereal—out of reach, the better. Perhaps we should tattoo this mantra on our forearms.

Getting from Point A to Point
"I Wish I Still Had a Car"

Let me begin by saying that I love public transportation. I haven't owned a car for nearly two years, but when I did have one, I had been reduced from a functioning human to a walking fly strip for tickets, fines, and citations. I am incapable of parking, driving, or being inside a car for fifteen minutes in any city without immediately accruing half of my net worth in bills to the city. So it is for the best—for me, not for the state and local governments who are undoubtedly losing half their revenue—that I am no longer behind the wheel.

That being said, riding in what are essentially petri dishes on wheels with every other Tom, Dick, and Harry to get to and from your daily activities can definitely get you down. Unless you are one of those people who have a beautiful, pristine bike that has essentially taken the position in your life usually reserved for first children, you're probably stuck with the rest of us schmucks. And just a word on said bicycles, because I am not referring to those of us who schlep ourselves around occasionally on bikeshares, because anyone who has ever used those things knows it is about as far from the actual city-biking experience as anything can be— but more on that later.

The point is, we know that people who take their biking seriously are going to (a) talk about it all the time, (b) be completely unaware that it has usurped their life entirely and turned them into an enormous douchebag in lycra, and (c) fill every social media outlet at their disposal with filtered photos of their precious two-wheeler in various city locations. These people are too good for public transportation, which is probably for the best, as the stench of smug self-satisfaction radiating off them would likely clog up any subway car.

So you generally have three options in terms of public transportation (and we'll consider trams and light rails and all that nonsense under the "metro" heading, because once you're inside one, they're essentially the same thing). You have the metro, or "subway" as many of you insist on calling it. You have buses. You have bikeshares. Now, all three can provide a safe, convenient, and rapid means of getting you where you need to go—though each have their definite pros and cons, and navigating them is essential to any young adult's survival.

THE METRO

Pros:

- Relatively fast, depending on the city.

- Affordable sometimes, especially in terms of how far you can travel in it.

- Underground, so you don't have to deal with the overwhelming grayness that can sometimes envelop cities.

- Pretty generous seating arrangements, depending on the city.

Cons:

• Consistently, overwhelmingly smells of urine. Reeks. Reeks of urine.

• Is for some reason considered an appropriate place by many amorous couples to get their "uncomfortable public makeout" quota filled.

• Is late all the time, just to fuck with you.

• Can vary in price on one metro in one day from "basically free" to "you could just break my kneecaps" (I'm looking at you, D.C.).

THE BUS

Pros:

• Sometimes you can find one that goes exactly where you want to go, in which case it's almost like a car you don't have to park.

• Extremely cheap.

• Above-ground, so it can sometimes be pleasant to sightsee on a bright, warm day.

• If you get a good seat, it is relatively comfortable.

Cons:

• You're riding the fucking bus, man. Doesn't that just sound bad?

• The bus is often where the crazies gather to sit next to you and eat a full chicken dinner/tell you about their many cats.

- If it's crowded, you're literally just bouncing around holding onto a strap as you barrel down an open road.

- The stops are outdoors, meaning if it's anything other than seventy degrees and sunny out, life is terrible.

THE BIKESHARE

Pros:

- Extraordinarily convenient, provided you start and finish near a station (that isn't always taken up).

- Beautiful on a nice day.

- Exercise, or whatever.

- Makes you feel cool, if even briefly.

Cons:

- You are never near a station—starting point or destination—and even if you are, they are entirely full 24/7.

- People apparently beat the bicycles mercilessly with a sledge-hammer every time they use them, judging by the state of most of them.

- They weigh approximately one zillion pounds.

- They have two gears: stuck in molasses or free-falling down a hill.

- No matter what the weather is or where you are going, you will arrive drenched in sweat.

Of the three, personally, I prefer the metro. But each is necessary in its own turn.

Regardless of your preference, not having a firm grasp on any and every form of public transportation at your fingertips is an unforgivable sin. It is often the difference between having the morning of a True Adult and flailing down the street with coffee spilled down your shirt as you come up with an excuse as to why you are late for the fourth time this week.

But I am convinced that this hurdle—learning how to start our days right from every angle—though one of the hardest, is one of the most essential. We always admired our parents for somehow getting everything together, being awake and aware, and even handing us a packed lunch all while we were trying to brush our teeth. Now is the time we should be learning how to make the most of our early day—or even be up to see it at all—because, let's face it: For every worm we're not going to get this morning, there are three perky white girls named Sophie who've already gotten three. We can't let Sophie win—we have to get our mornings in check.

FINDING AND KEEPING A JOB

Or, How to Make a Résumé the Right Mix of Lies and Actual Work Experience

Almost everything in life, from eating a sparse bowl of Trix (which they inexplicably turned from whimsical fruit shapes into colored balls), to paying your rent on time, requires money. And such is perhaps the most devastating realization of adulthood: If you want something, or need something, you're going to have to take care of it for yourself. The things that, as children, we always assumed just materialized in our homes—food, new clothes, dishwashing liquid, toilet paper— are the things that often sneak into your wallet while you're sleeping and abscond with the last $40 or so you have in your checking account. Worse yet, this money that is so essential to the living of daily life and the ability to do your laundry, eat food occasionally, and live in some kind of four-walled structure that prevents you from being rained on, has to be earned. We have to go out and get jobs, work at them every day for many hours a day, and wait for a check to come every two weeks. (I know, I was just as brokenhearted as you when I got this news.)

While the definition of *work* may be different for everyone, getting a job is something that even the most talented of freeloaders isn't going to be able to avoid forever. (Unless there is some magical land where unemployment checks never run out—Sweden, maybe?) As soon as we're spit out from whatever formal education we were pursuing, the stopwatch that is Unforgiving Life As an Adult starts running, and it is up to us to work our way through it. But how do we get jobs? And, more importantly, how do we carry them out every day, without exception, even when we're hungover?

The process is a complex one. From scanning endless want ads and job listings (of which you have a vague suspicion that at least 40 percent are fake), to creating a resume, to the interview, to eventually becoming Employee of the Month or some other such professional honor, there is nary a moment's rest. At all times, it is essential to stay as competitive and cutthroat as you can possibly be, edging out your competition by making your cover letter just 10 percent wittier, or 34 percent less needy-sounding. It doesn't take an economist to understand that hundreds of thousands of twentysomethings out there are essentially jousting to the death over criminally underpaid administrative assistant positions, and standing out from the crowd is essential to survival.

There are, of course, the more existential questions that will inevitably present themselves, the "Do I even want this stupid job?"–type crises of the career hunt. It's undeniable that a huge part of our motivation at the tender age of "I'm ready to be exploited in this unpaid internship" is the actual concept of having a job. Everyone wants you to land a "good" job—your parents, your more judgmental friends, all those ever-watching eyes on Facebook. But what actually constitutes a "good" job? It's more a vague image than anything else.

You probably wear nice-ish clothes, maybe a J. Crew blazer or some of the more sophisticated items at H&M. You have a morning

WHAT YOU DO
VS. WHAT YOU SAY YOU DO

Unpaid Intern	Assistant (to whatever job you want to do)
Unemployed	DJ and/or Blogger
Upscale Retail	Style Consultant
Administrative Assistant	Executive Assistant
MAC Store Worker	Makeup Artist
Literally Anything	Consultant
Apple Store Employee	The Second Coming of Jesus Himself

commute that takes a decent amount of time, but allows you to listen to your adult contemporary music or read your Kindle on the public transportation of your choice. You get to go to happy hours after work and socialize with other people wearing nice blazers, drinking pints of craft beer, and talking about things like *The Daily Show*, concerts you'd like to attend, and the various places within a twenty-mile radius that feature a nice brunch spread on Sundays. It's the kind of job your mother would be proud to tell her friends about, that allows you to report back to everyone with a fulfilled "I got my money's worth on this college thing" kind of smile, and that encourages you to open a—*shudder*—LinkedIn profile.

Of course, the best move would be to take a long time to actually consider what it is that you want to be doing in your life. Even within the relatively similar-looking world of Office Work™, there are a million and one variations on what it is you might actually end up doing. (We all grew up believing that people who put on nice clothes and went into an office all day were performing the universal task of writing a bunch of numbers into a giant book for "business purposes," but it turns out that isn't so!) Beyond that, it's quite possible that a nine-to-five career is not what you want to be dedicating most of your time and stress to for the next forty years. Maybe you want a job that leaves you a lot more breathing room on your off-hours to not stress about tomorrow's meeting and pursue a hobby, or raise kids, or socialize more. In that case, enjoy explaining to everyone you meet from now until the end of time that you didn't follow the path society was so hell-bent on having you take. If you do want one of those blazer-y jobs, however, your work is certainly cut out for you, especially in this economy.

First you have the hunt itself. Have you decided what you want to be doing? Have a dream career in mind? Good, now kindly ball that up (metaphorically, or you could actually write it on a piece of paper) and throw it out the window. Chances are that you're not going to find a full-time position teaching philosophy at an Ivy League school to only the best-looking students, complete with three months' paid vacation and a workweek that includes more hacky sack in the courtyard than actual office hours. And even if such an opening did exist, you're certainly not going to stumble onto it while browsing Monster.com. No, you're going to have to broaden your horizons and reduce your criteria to "nonlethal" and "within walking distance of a window." More or less, any office-related position should be appealing to you, as it includes air-conditioning, a break room, and the ability to cruise Wikipedia listlessly in the vast expanses of time when you haven't been assigned anything specific.

There are the usual hot spots for finding such jobs—especially if you're not picky about something entry-level or entry-level-adjacent—the classified ads, job fairs, the aforementioned Monster.com. And then you can turn to the less orthodox, if sometimes surprisingly efficient, employment databases, like Craigslist.

What is Craigslist, if not a cesspool of all our most base desires and unfiltered thoughts, collected together like scraps on the world's least-sanitary bulletin board, screaming out in all caps for someone like us to reach out and say that we're not alone? Putting a job posting on Craigslist is like saying, "Hey, I'm a risk taker, and understand that my future employee is either going to have a facial tattoo, or be twenty-three and know literally nothing about anything." No self-respecting forty-five-year-old who is looking to branch out into a different company in the same sector, interested in fielding a few offers and getting his name back out there, is going to browse Craigslist in his spare time while eating Cheetos and occasionally clicking over to YouPorn. CL is the bastion of those of us who aren't afraid to include things on our resume such as Highly Ranked Redditor and Founder/Editor-in-Chief, Seattle Food Blog.

The things you find lurking on sites like this—ones who include as many misleading links to phishing sites and porn as they do to actual job offers—can be as frustrating as they are endearing. Someone needs a secretary, doesn't have a great command of the shift key, and put her actual cell phone number out there to be contacted by whatever dregs of society might happen to be floating by the *Jobs: Full Time* section at four in the morning on a Tuesday. It's the kind of offer that is too uncoordinated to be fake, and, should you come across it during unforgiving day 534 of your job search, it looks like a succulent filet mignon after a hunger strike. You decide to send a general cover letter, and your resume, along with maybe a vaguely charming e-mail. And perhaps, in some alternate universe, that would be enough.

But this is today, in our world, and for every coffee bitch position available in an office in a big city, there are going to be at least five hundred twentysomethings clawing each other's eyes out to get it. So you have to be creative, be persistent, and stand out from the crowd. Once you've culled a list of potential jobs big enough to survive a 99.999 percent rejection rate and still land an interview or two, you can start honing the craft of making your presentation stand out from the tidal wave of other people with nearly identical qualifications. (If five hundred of you majored in history, participated in student government, and worked 2.3 internships in the past three years, it's going to require more than a saucy emoticon in the subject line of the e-mail to make you the candidate the hiring manager has to respond to.)

And how do you make yourself appear in a résumé to be twice the professional, thrice the charmer, and four times the international man of mystery than you are in real life?

It's simple: You lie.

Though perhaps not in the way you were told that lying would be when you were a child—all some clear-cut vision of "right" and "wrong," something that is either absolutely one thing or the other. As with many things in adulthood, you will find that life is a veritable tapestry of gray areas, each point as open to interpretation and tweaking as the next, and your job is to make all those blurry lines blur just enough in your favor. For example, saying that you attended two meetings of a planning committee for the Student Association in which your primary function was ensuring that at least some of the budget was getting siphoned into alcohol doesn't exactly scream "leadership skills." But presenting yourself as Student Advocate for Allocation of Funds sounds distinguished, and vague enough to be "probably pretty important" in the eyes of whoever is reading this.

Your internship? Downplay the part about taking people's lunch orders and emphasize the one day you got to sit in on a meeting with legitimate employees. Your special skills? There is no sport, hobby, or activity you cannot pretend you are way more talented and experienced in than you actually are. If you say "advanced salsa dancer," who is going to call you on that? Is the HR rep going to make you dance with her around the office like some busted version of the ballroom scene from *Beauty and the Beast*? No. So make it sound as if you're committed to something outside of work hours.

As for the interview itself, this is where all those nebulous-but-oh-so-desired "people skills" come in. And what exactly are all these vaunted people skills? As I understand the term, they include the following:

• Shaking someone's hand with the right combination of firm

and welcoming so that you appear to be neither challenging the person to an arm-wrestling match, nor offering the back of your hand to be kissed like some kind of Southern belle at a debutante ball. (It also helps if your palms do not have the humidity level of a terrarium.)

- Looking people in the eye when you talk to them, but not so much that you look like an infomercial salesman on hour nine of the all-night telethon.

- Being self-deprecating without being a Paul Giamatti character.

- Taking charge of situations, or at least appearing to take charge of them while you browse Wikipedia articles at your desk.

- Making light conversation that puts others at ease, and never feeling that terrifying need to keep talking when you're nervous that leads you to ultimately reveal the anxiety-induced constipation you've been battling leading up to the interview.

In reality, the interview will probably be pretty straightforward. You'll likely get questions thrown at you like, "What is your biggest flaw?" This is largely an opportunity for that irritating go-getter from middle school SGA to say something like, "Well, I guess you could say I'm a perfectionist," prompting everyone to projectile-vomit on each other.

You'll also be expected to discuss various aspects of your work experience, the kind of person you are, what your future goals might be, and other topics that you can essentially tap-dance over with Exactly What You Think They Want to Hear. The truth is, there are no right answers. It's just kind of a feeling that people get—the feeling that says, "This guy/gal is clearly the missing piece to our Accounts Receivable puzzle!" It's an instinct that cannot be explained by science, and is largely responsible for the inexplicable business success of utter toads like Donald Trump.

But what happens when you actually get the job? After clawing your peers' eyes out for the chance at an interview, only to all but promise your firstborn to get the job, it's hard not to feel mystified and more than a little nervous as to what to expect. The good news, however, is that there will be a few constants when it comes to workplace hazards. No matter where you go, you will always find four things: your best friend, your worst enemy, a reason you want to quit, and a reason you are terrified of actually quitting. Every job, in every sector, has these. What will they be? Based on my humble experience in the three major fields of work you might be getting into, I feel more than qualified to take you on a mini-tour of the Carnival of Horrors that awaits you.

Your Best Friend

FOOD SERVICE JOB

Here you will learn to love your drinking buddy. Since one of the major pluses of working in food service is not having to get up until around 2:00 p.m. (with the agonizing exception, perhaps, of Sunday brunches), going out after work for a few rounds is pretty much the professional sport of the restaurant world. Everyone likes to meet at an after-hours place, get shitty on Rumplemintz and whiskey, and get on the merry-go-round of casual sex partners the work environment provides. If you can find your own personal drinking bestie among the crew, you have found your savior. With her, you can gossip about coworkers, bitch about front-of-house bullshit, rag on customers, and cover each other's backs while you eat like a squirrel, crouched behind some refrigerator. In food service, a workplace best friend is indispensable.

OFFICE JOB

One thing that is often notably lacking in office work environments—something which food service tends to have in abundance—are people who can just kind of chill. They don't have to be the weed dealer of the HR department, but they should at least be able to shoot the shit and kick back at a decent happy hour. Oftentimes, the stress of the "let's-gouge-each-other's-eyes-out-to-get-ahead" work environment manifests in coworkers who are legitimately afraid of relaxing with one another, lest they get Brutus'd sometime in the middle of March when their guard is down. If your office doesn't have a cool person, I recommend suicide.

RETAIL JOB

If there is one thing that you need for a happy life in a retail environment, it is someone who is looking for shifts. It's 9:00 a.m., you went out drinking the previous night, you are too hungover to even look out the window, let alone go deal with eight hours of refolding stacks of T- shirts, and you are supposed to open the store in two hours. If you don't have a trusted colleague who is always looking to pick up some last-minute hours—you, sir (or ma'am, I don't know you), are nobody.

Your Worst Enemy

FOOD SERVICE JOB

You will undoubtedly encounter, during your time as a food service worker (whether you're spending it as a food runner, busboy, waiter, hostess, or—holy of holies—bartender), the dreaded Evil Manager. This is the person whose entire life is based on making the dining establishment a living hell for her employees, an endless labyrinth of redundant napkin folding and petty corrections over minor errors. For, you see, the Evil Manager has just the smallest, most lethal dose of power over a very concentrated pool of victims—and she is going to wield it in the fullest.

OFFICE JOB

There is one person who, no matter how much you enjoy your job or feel that you perform to a satisfactory degree in the eyes of your bosses, will make you want to wipe him off the planet with an oversized bottle of Windex: the go-getter. This is the person who consistently comes in way before it would be considered appropriate, leaves later than anyone else in the office, and is deliriously happy to take all that sweet, sweet extra work that no one else wants to do. The thing about an office environment is that it's a delicate balance of demonstrating what you can physically do as opposed to what it is realistic to do. Yes, technically, we could all come in at 6:00 a.m. and leave at midnight while taking some work home—but we shouldn't. However, if someone on the team takes it upon himself to prove that such a workload is, in fact, completely feasible—the rest of you are absolutely screwed.

RETAIL JOB

Your worst enemy here is the customer. You spend your days cleaning up after people who think that a dressing room is their own personal playpen in which to throw things around to amuse themselves, and the products you've so lovingly arranged are there to be destroyed at their leisure.

Why You Want to Quit

FOOD SERVICE JOB

Because spending all day staring at people eating delicious-looking food that you have zero time to eat, all while living off tips that some customers seem to get a kind of sadistic thrill out of cheating you on, can become grating after a while. It's clear that some people get sucked into the relatively easy money of tips and find themselves, long after they'd hoped to move on to something that doesn't leave them smelling like bacon/a deep fryer at the end of the day, locked into expenses that they can only cover with a good Friday night shift.

OFFICE JOB

Despite all the societal benefits that an office job undoubtedly provides, it also often leaves you with a feeling of perpetually being at work. There is always something more that can be done—a project to polish, an e-mail to send, research to do—and you know that for every minute you just chill out watching TV and eating take-out Thai food, some insufferable go-getter a few cubicles down is efficiently squirreling away lots of extra work to bring in and show the bosses the following morning. The job, in some ways, begins to infiltrate and consume other aspects of your life—as it is often considered "not a job, but a career" (i.e., something that you are expected to sacrifice a normal social/romantic life to get ahead in).

RETAIL JOB

There are relatively few fulfilling aspects of a retail job, to be honest. The money is often decent, but never good. You have few options for upward mobility. The customers, as previously mentioned, are egregious. Oftentimes, stores will give you a discount that is just high enough to keep you spending your whole paycheck on their overpriced products. The daily grind of this tends to wear on you, until you have a hard time thinking of any job in the entire world—including the person who scoops up horse poop at rich people's farms—as less enticing for one reason or another.

Why You're Not Going to Quit

FOOD SERVICE JOB

The tips. The sweet, sweet tips.

OFFICE JOB

Once you get sucked into an office job—and by that, I mean you've invested enough of your soul to make it seem like a part of your life, the way another human being might be—there is a sense of obligation about it. You've already climbed, say, six rungs up the corporate ladder (and had to step on the faces of some decent people along the way), so why would you bail out now? Office jobs often have a tendency to define you, as they have the unfortunate reputation of being "your real job." People in the service industries will often talk about how they're just making money while they wait to find the real thing, and once you get a lock on said actual job, it's hard to let it go. You are no longer just "Sarah, blond girl and skilled maker of pancakes," you are, "Sarah, blond marketing director for That Company Over There." Even if we end up hating it, it has often crept into too much of who we are as a person to just drop it.

RETAIL JOB

The discount, though not enough to keep you locked behind a cash register on its own, is part of an overall comfort zone you can easily slip into when working retail. The money is just enough not to be bad, usually, and the job is often so easy that leaving it seems like more trouble than it's worth. The tired complacency that leads us to stay in shitty retail positions for extended periods of time is something that should have its own pharmaceutical to combat.

So, as you see, every job you can possibly hope to have in life is going to have its ups and downs. Sometimes you might feel as though the entire professional world is conspiring against you. The important part is finding a life outside of work that fulfills, excites, and challenges you, because there are few things worse than having an identity entirely wrapped up in and defined by something that you can one day get fired from. We've all had brunch with those people who are incapable of talking about anything except their workweeks and various interesting things that happened to them with colleagues you've never heard of and/or don't care about, and we know how tedious it is for everyone else, so it goes without saying that this should be avoided.

But having a job is essential to life, and no matter how we choose to spend our working hours, we're going to need to do something. Maybe, in order to maximize the amount of enjoyment we get out of working versus how many nights we go home and bang our heads repeatedly against the wall, we should come up with some kind of checklist for jobs we should be looking for. What is important, though? What are the deciding factors for what is going to make a job both attainable and fulfilling? Assuming that the world is just a sparkly merry-go-round of perfect jobs to pick from, what are the qualities that you could ultimately forgo in order to be happy overall?

There are those among us who put top priority on our social lives. For those folks, it is essential to go out and stay out late, to try new things, to make friends, to be "on the scene" —whatever "scene" that may be. Regardless of who is going to condescendingly talk to you about how you're "getting a little old for this nonsense," your goal in life is to have a rich social calendar filled with activities and fabulous people and the errant bottle of champagne opened with a sword. Guess what, though? A huge number of jobs kind of cut that lifestyle off at the knees.

We all think, on some level, that we can beat the system when it comes to balancing work life and play life. And, yes, a couple coke-fueled, completely fucking insane traders working at some huge investment bank in Manhattan manage to pull off eighty-hour workweeks and six-hour benders at clubs—but you are not one of them. And, plus, have you met them? Or, God forbid, worked with them? Because I have. (Met one, not worked with one. I'm happy to say that I've never held a job sucking the blood out of little children's dreams at some Patrick Bateman–filled investment bank.) And you know what they're like in person? Horrifying. At least the ones I've met. I was once lucky (?) enough to have an in-depth conversation with one of those fabled worka-holic financiers about the circus-esque logistics of his life and the realities of having such immense professional pressure at the age of twenty-five. This was essentially our exchange:

Me: So you must work really long hours, don't you?

Him: Yeah, we usually get into work at around 8:00 a.m. and don't leave until at least nine-ish. Sometimes we're there until midnight or whatever, it really depends.

Me: Damn! How do you have time to do other things?

Him: We go out and party all the time. I would say at least a few nights a week we go out to a club and stay there until 5:00 a.m. or so.

Me: And you're not tired?

Him: I'm tired all the time! Are you kidding? But that's just part of the lifestyle, kind of.

Me: Do you even have time for a girlfriend?

Him: Kind of. Most of the guys who work at the bank date girls who work in the fashion industry because they also work crazy hours, and they get paid shit, and they're usually gorgeous—it goes pretty well with the lifestyle. Plus, they don't really have a chance of moving up in their field, so they usually quit around thirty to become housewives. Pretty much all the guys do it.

Me: So why do you do this job?

Him: Are you kidding? You don't want to know how much money I make, but it's a lot. A lot.

Obviously, this is just one guy telling his rather extreme story (though I should mention that I later interviewed a pretty prominent fashion blogger who confirmed for me that she and many friends in the industry date almost exclusively within the financial industry), but it illustrates some of the problems we all face. There is a balance to be struck somewhere between enjoying your work, making a good living, and having time to do other things. And unless you're doing a shit ton of coke (which this guy didn't mention but which seems like a crucial element to the story, if you ask me), it's not really possible to have all three at the same time. So being the "social life" guy may mean choosing a job that is either in an industry that permits it (such as the food industry), or one that has relatively light workloads, which allow you a comfortable ten-to-five workday and no projects to take home and obsess over at the end of the day.

If you're the kind of person who wants to make a lot of money, that would seem more straightforward, wouldn't it? I mean, hey, I'm not here to judge you for your Monopoly Man-esque ambitions. I can respect the desire to live comfortably and buy a new Apple product every two weeks without thinking twice about it. So why don't you just find a job that is really lucrative, work really hard at it, climb some invisible corporate ladder, and reap the benefits? Apparently, it doesn't work like that. We know that the idea of "working really hard" being directly proportional to exactly how much you will succeed is incredibly untrue in practice (no matter what you say, old white Republican males, no one will ever believe your success was 100 percent self-made). But it's also important to note that well-paying jobs are kind of hard to locate in the first place.

I think the job market is now officially aware that we're all desperate. As I mentioned before, for every ad that shows up on Craigslist for some underpaid secretarial post, there are going to be about five hundred motivated twentysomethings with master's degrees ready to get into the octagon and kill each other with their bare hands to get it. And this is only a slight exaggeration; people are desperate. What does a company stand to gain from paying someone a really good wage when they could get away with paying half of it and still have someone who basically bursts into happy tears every lunch break over his profound luck to have found this job? People are accepting lower and lower salaries for jobs that, if the economy weren't such a clusterfuck, they never would have accepted in the first place.

But what could be improved, pretty easily, is the lifestyle that goes with your job. Unless you happen to stumble upon one of the few industries left that is still throwing an expense account at every intern with good hair, you are going to have to manage your day-to-day life around it. First and foremost, don't live in an expensive city. I hate to say it, because the whole world is basically screaming, *"If you don't live in New York City, you aren't worthy of life on this planet, you peasant,"* but that shit is a privilege. I mean, really, we all know people who moved to The City with not a whole lot in the way of plans or connections but a vague idea of "making it." You know what they end up doing? Waiting tables, bartending, or working in a store—or possibly several of those at the same time. You know what kind of life that affords you in a city as ball-crushingly expensive as New York? A terrible one. I mean, yeah, technically you can scrape by and talk about how you're "high on the energy of the city," but you're certainly not going to afford being high on anything else.

There are so many other places you could be, both around America and around the world at large that would enable you to balance out your financial life a little more. And, in the interest of full disclosure, I did live in Paris myself when I didn't have a fancy grown-up job, but I was a student, working as an au pair (a glorified nanny), and lived in one hundred square feet. Do you know what one hundred square feet looks like? It is unfortunate and in no way allows you to fully enjoy The City for all the majesty it has to offer you. You don't want to be toiling away in that lifestyle when you're nearing thirty.

And as to a job you enjoy, there is a good chance that landing one will severely damage your social life potential, as well as any chance of highly lucrative compensation. We often see people who are "married to their work," and that means exactly what it sounds like. They are always spending excessive time with it, sacrificing everything else for it, and generally being defined by it. A lot of people who work in the more "glamorous" professions, such as the arts or PR or TV production, tend to be of this persuasion. They would essentially give at least two of their appendages to have more professional success, and everything about them tends to center on how well their job has been going lately. It's pretty clear with a lot of this group—from the DJ/web designer in a rotating carousel of Snapbacks, to the writer who has an impressive résumé of prestigious bylines that don't actually pay—that the money is not always overflowing to compensate them for the effort. Speaking personally, as a writer, every time you ever announce that you work in such a profession, you are immediately met with an open look of smug disbelief and a demand for further clarification.

Or, if you are being fairly paid, it often comes at the expense of any time out and about. There comes a moment in many of these "passion" jobs when, at two in the morning on a Friday night, when you're still hard at work on a project that you are putting extra time in without having been asked to (and with no prospect of compensation), where you sort of take a long, hard look at your life and wonder how exactly you came to be "that guy." None of us wants to feel like we have sacrificed a balanced, fun life for being the MVP at work several months in a row. Regardless of how much money we might make, or how admired we may be by our coworkers, it certainly seems as if we must live a pretty pointless life. So if you are in hot pursuit of a job that makes your heart go all aflutter, it may behoove you to resign yourself to at least a few years of being Career Guy, even if you hate to admit it.

No matter what you are looking for in your job, or what you end up doing, it's only important that it makes you happy. It could be bringing in ample money, giving you a super-flexible schedule, or simply making you feel as if you accomplished something at the end of the day. It could be the job of your dreams or just something that provides you with money to travel to all your various fetish conventions around the country. At the end of the day, you're the one who has to sit on your bed, take off your shoes, and think about what you accomplished (as well as what lies ahead of you). And if it makes you hate your life and everything about it, or makes you question your worth even a little bit, you should probably pull up your résumé and start fluffing it up, because you've got some applications to fill out.

Chapter 3

HOBBIES

Or, How to Find Things to
Do That Don't Depend
Entirely on Drinking

First and foremost, what is a hobby? So many of us go from the ages of birth to twenty-two-ish without ever having taken that into consideration. It's a word that has general meaning (something you do for enjoyment in your spare time), but throughout much of our early lives, the concepts of both enjoyment and spare time were rather vague. We knew that there were fun things we could be doing, and we might have had an idea of which things interested us more than others, but we didn't have a whole lot of control over things like transportation, finances, and extracurricular education. For everything from breakdance lessons to showing everyone up at the middle school Spring Fling to the errant trip to Chuck E. Cheese, we were at the whim of our guardians.

Think about it: You're a kid, and you're hardly capable of making a decision as important and influential on the trajectory of the rest of your life as "What am I going to do with all this spare time that I, as a six-year-old, am faced with?" So your parents will usually fill in those blanks for you: Enjoy your five-ish years of ballet, soccer, karate, or gymnastics. Maybe Little League, if your family is more old-school. The point is, the activity is going to be pretty straightforward, it will be planned with the precision of a Swiss timepiece, and you aren't going to have a whole lot of say in the matter. (If you happen to have often-written-about-when-analyzing-the-downfall-of-our-generation Helicopter Parents, enjoy doing all these activities at once, on an incredibly strict schedule, while your twitchy, forceful elders live vicariously through your tiny successes in hopes that you will prove to be "gifted.")

And then, as if by magic, you're in high school, where your extracurricular activities start flying fast and free. (Or maybe even middle school, if you've actually started caring about college applications at age twelve, but chances are that period of your life doesn't get into full swing until around sophomore year.) Now is the time to pick activities that, in addition to potentially being enjoyable on their own merits, are guaranteed to make you look like a "well-rounded teenager" whose activities include things outside of scowling at people at the mall and drinking Red Bulls, like the majority of your teenage peers. And while *well-rounded* is certainly a term that sounds positive in theory, in practice, it can end up even more insufferable than the aforementioned scowling mall-hangers. It's a tough balance to strike, being productive and still having a normal childhood, and not everyone manages it.

If you were an admissions officer at a prestigious university with a good balance between party life and rigorous academics, imagine what you would want to see on an application. Things like student government, sports, drama—and anything in which you can exaggerate a position of take-charge leadership. Nothing says, "I made the most out of my three-week stint in debate club" like treasurer. Engaging in hobbies in high school (without becoming an insane, Tracy Flick-esque, type A personality whom everyone avoids like the plague) is a direct step toward a better future, with a relatively high return on investment. You're not just participating in these tedious student association meetings for yourself, you're participating in them for your grandchildren, and for the future they deserve from your getting into a highly ranked state school.

In college, hobbies are so very many things. Never in your life do you have such a potent combination of free time, youth, access to social events, and tingling loins that long to meet other, similar-minded sexy young people in various activities. This is the time to get involved politically for about ten minutes, to try out for a play (even though you've never been in the same room as a stage) simply because the person you're trying to bang is a huge drama nerd. There is nothing you can't do when faced with such a lascivious Roman orgy of potential social groups and time-consuming activities. And, better still, nothing really counts in terms of social repercussions. You don't have to be labeled so swiftly and cruelly by your choice of activity, the way you are in high school. You can dabble in a little of everything— including recreational drug use—without being defined by it. *Everything* is a hobby.

But when you graduate, when you are spit out into the world in which 90 percent of people with whom you come in contact are your coworkers or crappy neighbors, what are you supposed to do? How do you continue to dedicate time to things that do not provide you with money and, at least directly, do not contribute to your future? How do you just sign up for something for "fun," and do it—especially when it isn't centered around the consumption of alcohol? It seems intimidating to say the least, especially given how limited our free time is at this age. You come home at the end of a ten-hour workday, and the last thing you want to do is go to a pottery class at which you are going to struggle to make something even vaguely blob-shaped as fellow grown-ass adults snicker under their breath at your incompetence.

It does seem exhausting, and the chances are high that you could end up making a fool of yourself more than anything else when it finally comes time to show up and participate, but the benefits certainly outweigh the risks. Think about it: You will be meeting new people who don't work two cubicles down from you; you will potentially have a different pond in which to insert (tee-hee) your fishing rod and scavenge for romantic partners; and you may even learn something in the process (cue inspirational music). If you are feeling the ever-tighter grip of limited social options as a young adult in the working world, few things are more liberating than giving yourself a new outlet for hanging out.

But which hobby is for you? There are so many different aspects of personal growth and enjoyment that a hobby can fulfill—it really depends on what you're looking for. Generally, it's best to pick three or four from a list of things that you want to get out of your new activity. The range of possibilities, at least in my humble experience, looks something like this:

- Losing a certain amount of weight/getting in shape without having to go to the gym and be stared at by grunting, flexing bros and hot soccer moms in full makeup on the elliptical.

- Meeting a new group of friends who will at least somewhat extricate you from your incestuous inner circle of people who cannot stop sleeping with, dating, and breaking up with each other at regular intervals.

- Staving off having to sign up for online dating for at least a few more months with the hope that you're going to meet the love of your life between the hours of 7:30 and 8:30 p.m. after work three days a week.

- Potentially honing a skill that you would one day perhaps like to turn into a full-time career (a career that doesn't make you vaguely consider suicide every time the alarm goes off).

- Being able to tell people you meet about your exciting new activity, briefly giving the illusion that you are a multifaceted human being with interests outside of browsing the Internet for GIFs of cats and taking Photo Booth pictures of yourself holding a glass of wine.

- Reconnecting with a friend or significant other by engaging in some new, fun thing with her that doesn't include eating handfuls of cheddar popcorn and watching reality television (not that those things aren't uplifting and wonderful).

- Learning a new skill that you've always thought of as being really cool and something that, despite the likelihood that you will be terrible at it, you really want to try.

No one hobby is going to cover all these bases, and that's fine—you probably don't need it to. But opening the door to having things to do throughout your week besides working, sleeping, and eating Chinese food is guaranteed to bring nearly endless other possibilities of things you could engage in. The guy at your office who is training for a marathon, who comes in with his bike hoisted above his head, who is constantly attending these obscure jazz concerts and telling you about the amazing group of Czech backpackers he hosted through Couchsurfing—how do you think he got that way? Do you think he just woke up one morning and said to himself, "Hey, I think I'm going to make all the people I come in contact with feel bad about their total lack of motivation in life?" I mean, it's possible, but I doubt it. It's a process, and it has to start somewhere.

Getting Involved in Activities

First things first: You're probably going to want to get in shape. Now, as someone whose fingertips are at least 70 percent of the time coated in a thin film of Dorito dust, I am not one to decide exactly what "in shape" should entail. It is not a particular size, it is not a particular diet, but it is a feeling. Even I, who would literally subsist on a diet of whipped cream shots out of the can and curly fries if given the opportunity, have had to suck it up and balance my life out a little bit. Does that mean giving up everything that's seen the business end of a deep fryer forever? No. Does it mean spending all your spare time doing hot yoga while feeling incredibly inadequate/sweaty? No. But it does mean finding a decent middle ground, and a good group activity can always help with this.

Let's say you join a dance class. Yes, at first you're going to look ridiculous and probably gross out countless partners with your extreme Clammy Hand Syndrome brought on by crippling nervousness. It happens. And it's tough, because becoming suddenly aware of how out-of-shape and uncoordinated you are can tend to cancel out your potential dates motivation for signing up in the first place. But as time goes on, and as you start to realize that moving your body around occasionally can make your whole day go by smoothly and be filled with more energy, it begins spilling over into the rest of your life.

You want to eat a little better, you want to maybe take the stairs instead of the elevator, you want to make the small changes throughout your day that make getting out on the dance floor (and into a relatively attractive dancing outfit) less of a Sisyphean undertaking. Whatever form of physical activity seems least painful to you, go for it. The point is not so much *what* you're doing, it's *that* you're doing something. Because unless you start to put the occasional green thing in your mouth and leave the sitting/lying position for at least thirty minutes a day, you're not going to have much energy for anything else.

There is no rule that says you have to join a club to get into shape. You could very easily start jogging in your neighborhood and keeping a food log that puts into brutally clear terms just how many Swiss Cake Rolls your daily routine consists of. But if your goal is also to start a new activity during which you come in contact with new people/change up your lifestyle, it is killing two very large birds with one relatively inexpensive stone. There are a lot of benefits to choosing a hobby that includes physical exertion—but that doesn't mean it isn't without its downsides.

Each potential activity you could undertake has its own very distinct pros and cons, and it is best to be aware of them from the get-go. If we're being honest with ourselves, we'll acknowledge that most of us will probably attempt a few big ones for two weeks before abandoning them in favor of more frequently attending happy hours, and we need to address those. If you are going to pick up something obscure, like Tuvan Throat Singing, I commend you—but as I have no information on the subject, I'll just assume it's nothing but upsides. Bitches love a Tuvan Throat Singer.

LEARNING A NEW LANGUAGE

Pros:

- You are learning something that gives you a very direct and tangible ability, one you can use as you learn it and practice on your own time, as opposed to things like salsa dancing or fly fishing, which are hard to put in hours for while your unamused roommate tries to play Xbox next to you.

- It's relatively inexpensive, especially considering all the Rosetta Stones that are out there for the illegal downloading—I mean purchasing, like a decent human being.

- If you get good enough that your meet-up groups can include actual native speakers, this could be the opportunity to meet hot, foreign tail. And even at the beginner meetings, you are at least guaranteed a group of potential dates who have a vague interest in culture.

- Learning another language provides even more justification for your already ill-advised vacation, at which you know upwards of 80 percent of your time will be spent drinking with other English speakers.

Cons:

• It's among the least physically engaging activities you can take up, so any hopes of burning off the extra wine calories drunk at meet-ups is out the window, unless you hold your speaking groups while riding tandem bicycles.

• The groups of adults learning/practicing languages are often peppered with at least a small sprinkling of creepers who are solely there to hit on people (and don't even try to mask it with a vague attempt at the language).

• Come on, it's a little nerdy.

• In order to take the language-learning experience to its proper level (and to reward yourself for all the hours spent practicing), you're eventually going to have to schlep yourself to a foreign country where it's actually spoken—an investment that counteracts any amount of language workbooks you may have stolen off the Internet.

PARTNER DANCING

Pros:

• This exercises both literal muscles and the tender emotional muscles that are flexed by having to come in constant, repeated contact with strangers.

• You are learning a skill that is undoubtedly useful, as there is nothing worse than being the person at a wedding or other

YOUR STANDARD CREEPER

Fedora

Gelled hair

Unerring gaze at all the
young women in the room

Short-sleeve
"cool guy"
button-down shirt

Sweaty palms

Crotch which is
always mysteriously
too close to others
during dance lessons

Smartphone with Reddit
as the homepage

Stains on jeans
from rubbing palms

Nervously shaking leg

event that requires dancing and refusing to step on the dance floor for fear of "looking stupid." That person never gets laid.

- Being able to dance will help you in your seduction of potential mates when you're out and about, since nothing is sexier than someone who can do a dance that doesn't involve having a set of genitals rhythmically grind against your lower back.

- Your butt will look like two scoops of butter pecan ice cream in your clingy dance clothes if you stick religiously to your practice regimen.

Cons:

- You have to dance in front of actual people, and since you are going to see them on a regular basis, you can't just humiliate yourself willy-nilly.

- Sweaty dance trolls who are there solely to foist themselves on unsuspecting students lurk in the corner of every dance hall, and you may be forced to come in contact with them during the partner-rotating portion of the lesson.

- Possible financial investment in dancing shoes so you're not the "guy wearing running shoes at the dance lesson."

- As soon as you make it known that you have taken up partner dancing to any degree, you are automatically labeled "dancing person," who is expected to "bust out moves" at any and all occasions, even if you are severely unprepared to show off the things you've learned. "Come on, twirl me around" will be the new mantra of everyone who has consumed more than one and a half beers within ten feet of you.

BOOK READING OR WRITING CLUB

Pros:

- You will be welcomed into the elite-yet-clammy world of "intellectuals" who actually devote their free time to reading real books, often printed on actual paper. Though anachronistic, it is surely your entry ticket into a more classy caste of society.

- You'll be provided with a list of literature to read, so you no longer have to do the searching and self-motivating to plow through the new Jonathan Franzen tome.

- You get a chance to meet bookish hotties who can sport a dapper cardigan and horn-rimmed glasses and would be happy to retire to bed after a few glasses of red and a conversation about Bukowski over Indian food.

- You belong to a group that motivates you to work on all that terrible poetry you've been saving up in your cramped little heart space for all these years—the poetry that the world doesn't even know it's missing.

Cons:

- If getting healthy were even a peripheral goal of yours in taking up a new hobby, sitting around reading/writing/talking about books with other doughy hipsters in blazers is hardly the most efficient strategy.

- The reading could potentially be bad/uninteresting—or you could just be incredibly lazy—and you may find yourself at a meeting for which you have not done the appropriate preparation. You will essentially be re-creating the bullshitting of your tenth-grade term paper on *The Grapes of Wrath*, only this time, it's your chosen leisure activity.

- You stand to discover how terrible your poetry actually is.

- People may expect you to be more articulate/thoughtful/ informed now that you have taken up reading as your personal activity, which could lead to awkward watercooler discussions when it is discovered that, outside the book of the month, you mostly just read your Facebook feed.

TEAM SPORTS

Pros:

- The overall benefits of having to work with peers in a team setting to achieve a common goal is one we readily acknowledge with children, but we often forget how positive it can be for adults as well.

- Teamwork is still a good experience at twenty-five.

- You may get to wear cute uniforms, uniforms that potentially show off the adorable butts of some of your cuter teammates.

- An automatic sense of unity and friendship is forged within the group, which greatly facilitates after-game recreation—a useful quality, as the transition from meet-up group to genuinely fun happy hour is not always a smooth one.

- You may actually burn a calorie or two while you're having a good time.

Cons:

- You run a high risk of getting sweaty, which is not the most conducive quality when you want to flirt with your fellow athletes.

- Adult recreational sports always involve a vague silliness—all of us run a little like wonks, move somewhat slowly, and generally don't look at the top of our game. It can be unsettling to those of us especially prone to embarrassment over our appearance.

- The uniforms might be highly unflattering.

- There is almost guaranteed to be a Team Asshole whose sole purpose is showing everyone else how athletic and talented he is, which begs the question, "Why are you playing adult recreational sports when you could clearly be out at the Olympics with your more qualified peers?"

The different kinds of hobbies we can take up as adults are almost limitless (even if they usually fall into a few general categories). No matter what your goals are, or where you live, with the advent of the Internet, you can do almost anything with your spare time if you are looking for something besides binge drinking. If you want to pop balloons for sexual release, there is a group for you—and you may get your very own voyeuristic special on TLC. If you enjoy dressing up as anthropomorphic cartoon animals and running around convention halls taking pictures of each other, you likely have a meet-up in your area this week. If you like going out into wooded areas and taking pictures of wildlife to note in some adorable little journal like you're ten years old, you have endless options out there.

But whatever you choose to dedicate your time to, you have to find something. Because we have all likely met that guy who has so thoroughly clung to the collegiate lifestyle, basing all life's significant moments and unallocated time to drinking or, in a more general sense, "partying." While there is definitely a certain charm in being the most efficient binge drinker in the tristate area when you're nineteen, that title gains a tinge of sadness when you're well into your twenties.

Obvious health implications for your poor, innocent liver aside, there are distinct limitations in a lifestyle that is wholly centered around being perpetually inebriated. You'll only meet certain kinds of people, go certain places, and you'll have to face the inevitable fear of socializing while completely sober and 100 percent yourself. For some, the idea of integrating a new daily/weekly activity that may cost money, doesn't come with free drinks, and is based on learning a skill seems foreign at best, terrifying at worst. It's just not something we're used to.

Taking up a new activity for the first time can be terrifying; it requires stepping out of the comfort zone of "hanging out" that we never even considered before. It's disarming at first, how much joining a group makes us all feel like children again—afraid to embarrass ourselves and constantly on the verge of nervous tears.

I remember the first time I went to a real swing dance class (a hobby that would end up becoming a big part of my life), I was fucking terrified. First of all, I've always been a pretty uncoordinated human being. It's not that I'm not graceful, as much as I'm essentially a human version of those crazy inflatable dancing car dealership guys. I just kind of flop and wiggle around like an overcooked noodle, knocking things over and spilling things on myself. And, true to form, I was terrible at first. I couldn't remember the steps, I had a hard time letting other people lead me, and I had hilariously poor form. It was just a mess, and for hours at a time, I would feel the creeping, burning feeling on the back of my neck of a bunch of randos watching me humiliating myself for their enjoyment.

Even worse, the entire group seemed like high school 2.0, in that everyone was already paired off, cliqued up, and designated into "cool" versus "not cool." The people who were really good dancers were in their own little world, completely unaffected by the plebians over in our corner trying to learn not to step on their own feet every time they turned. It seemed like an impenetrable world of talent and friendship and preestablished groups. But as with most things, as we get more familiar with an environment, it tends to lose some of its initial, terrifying luster. It became more understandable, I started to really dance, and the once-intimidating groups suddenly revealed themselves as standard-issue Dance Nerds who were just really cool in their one environment. Outside of that—at a party, for example—they were as awkward and strange as everyone else. And considering how much partying serves to unify even the most diverse groups of friends and hobbyists, it was hilarious to see them so completely out of their element.

We come to rely on the act of partying as a social lubricant that allows us to do—and attempt to have sex with—whatever we want. And there's nothing wrong with partying; it's awesome. But let's not act as though the actual definition of a *party* itself doesn't drastically change the further away from higher education we get. There are only so many times you can initiate a round of beer pong on a Tuesday night before all your nine-to-five friends start looking at you as "that guy." This isn't to say that we should all resign ourselves to the slippery descent into going home at 10:00 p.m. on a Friday night and shooting judgmental looks at our friends who want to enjoy a tiny slice of nightlife before they wither and die, but it's all about balance.

And nothing helps strike that balance better than finding something constructive to do with your spare time. Speaking from personal experience, you may encounter friends or coworkers who regard your decision to join a dance group or go to language meetups or book clubs with more than a slight raise of the eyebrow.

"What's this?" they seem to gasp with flustered incredulity, monocle popping out and landing neatly in their champagne glass full of Coors Light. "You mean you actually have little activities you go to? How cute!" The truth is that as young adults we are just not acquainted with the concept of voluntarily signing up for shit that isn't going directly on a college application or resume. What do you stand to gain, except possibly a noticeable dip in your checking account from monthly fees?

In all honesty, you stand to gain a lot.

We put huge premiums, when dating or seeking new friends, on people who are "cultured." When setting up an OKCupid account, we know that we don't want some toothless yokel who dislikes gay people on principle and has never left his hometown. But why don't we want these things? If we're being honest, we probably want someone who is able to expand our horizons and possibly teach us—I know, teach?! Us?!? But we're the smartest people in the world!—something new. We want someone who is full of diverse interests and has filled his spare time with activities both enriching and challenging. Who wants to be with someone who is totally complacent in an unironic Dale from *King of the Hill* kind of way?

And yet, we often don't demand this of ourselves. We picture our ideal best friend or significant other, and imagine someone who is able to integrate seamlessly into every gathering, from a pretentious book release party filled with faux intellectuals and professors tenured enough to openly hit on their more attractive pupils, to a round of foosball in a dive bar in which every surface is inexplicably sticky. But are we able to do those things? Most likely the answer is no, even if we would describe ourselves on dating sites or on a first date as "pretty cultured." No one wants to admit that a vast majority of her free time is spent giggling at the neckbeards on the MRA sections of Reddit and chilling out with their cats—it's just not sexy.

In order to break the cycle of no one actually doing anything interesting but everyone wanting someone with a little panache, we have to take the first step. And even if your motivation for signing up for that new club is specifically to sleep with higher and higher echelons of society, who cares? You'll probably eventually get something more enriching or interesting out of the experience. You'll meet people you would never have met in the dark recesses of a nightclub. And you'll have something interesting to discuss at the next get-together among friends who are still firmly stuck in their Netflix–and–Chinese food quicksand. But you have to take that first step.

Go online. Find meet-up groups. Ask a friend who is heavily involved in salsa dancing or her adult-education painting classes. Get over your fear of looking ridiculous by acknowledging that everyone looks as ridiculous as you in the beginner class. Invest the little bit of money it takes initially and understand that not every dollar you spend is going to buy something completely tangible. Be your own motivational poster. Become that insufferable asshole at work who is always doing something fun and interesting and meeting new people. You can do it.

Chapter
4

GOING OUT

Or, How to Justify
a $12 Cocktail
by Screaming
"This Is My Song!"

L et's go out. Are there any three words that simultaneously mean so much and so little as these? If you're in your twenties, it's pretty much a guarantee that your friends, potential dates, or significant others are going to be hounding you to "go out" and ostensibly make the most of your evening every single night. Monday, your best friend got an office job, so you have to hit a club. Tuesday, someone got fired, so you have to commiserate over happy hour. Wednesday, everyone is hitting dollar draft nights at that bar that won't stop playing "These Boots Were Made for Walking" as though that were ever a good song. Thursday has been Thirsty Thursday since you were sixteen goddamn years old. Friday is date night. Saturday night has open bar at that pretentious lounge until eleven. Sunday is for the Bloody Mary brunch that somehow bleeds into early Monday morning. It's inescapable.

Of course, you can't say yes to all of these; you would die either of alcohol poisoning or starvation from no longer being able to afford to feed yourself. It's simply not an option, and even if you're getting taken out on a date one or two nights a week, it's not going to offset the cost of dancing in a circle with your friends the nights before and after. It's simply not an option to do it all at once. And, let's be honest, we can't quite go out the way we used to. It's tough but necessary to admit for a twentysomething that we're "young" but we're not "that young," and constant binge drinking with friends is among the first things to get hacked off that list.

It's fairly easy to get stuck in the social quicksand of going out every night to drink; it's an obvious, universally accessible way to get everyone together and hanging out. It also enables everyone to be well-lubricated and capable of engaging in the various shenanigans and hijinks they won't permit themselves in the unforgiving light of day. And despite the insistence of many bars on charging upwards of $12 per cocktail, it can often be fairly affordable. But even if you're drinking at someone's house and therefore spending less on your night out than you would seeing a single movie, it is clearly unhealthy to find yourself constantly drinking every time the clock strikes five.

On the other hand, nights alone with take-out Thai, a rerun of your favorite TV show, and browsing Tumblr for vegan recipes to laugh at aren't going to be cute seven nights a week, either. Clearly, you need to strike a balance, but no one's there to tell us where to set the limits. If we listened to our parents, we would never leave the house except to go to work, on bike rides, or to check out a new museum exhibit that doesn't interest us. If we listened to our "party friends," we would probably be addicted to crystal meth by now. If we accepted all the invites in our OKCupid inbox, we would become a less appealing version of a Katherine Heigl movie, perpetually rolling our eyes at lame first dates. (And/or we would become those heinous semihumans who literally only accept dates in order to exploit an unsuspecting suitor to get a free dinner, but those people are monsters, and you're all cool and perfect.) There are many things we could be doing with our social calendar, and even with such pressing options on all sides, the balance can be struck.

As I mentioned before, we face a palpable divide in our twenties between those of us who have "real, big kid" jobs, and those of us who are left bowing at the altars of tips and retail. And though it is pretty clear that the "cool" ones—at least the ones able to look at friends with a subtle mix of pity and disdain at brunches—are the ones with professional jobs, this is one category in which they undoubtedly lose. Though having a professional job may provide you with the kind of disposable income that allows you to frequent clubs and lounges called Love/Hate or the Blue Room, it certainly doesn't leave you with the ability to sleep afterward. Having to wake up at 7:00 a.m. every morning for a commute, followed by eight hours in meetings and in front of computer screens doesn't exactly leave you wanting to scream at each other over David Guetta songs at the end of the day. Friends who work in the service industry, however, will be down as a clown to hit the after-hours club directly after their shift, and can do as many lines in the bathroom as they want, because their alarms are set the next day for a robust 4:00 p.m.

Undoubtedly the worst combination of these two is working at a coffee shop. Having done stints at two of them myself, I can say with confidence that not only does it leave you doing a job pretty soundly shit on by society at large, but it also requires you to wake up at 4:00 a.m. to start the morning shift. Why should any human being have to wake up at 4:00 a.m.? It's the absolute worst in terms of sleep cycles, because it's not working the night shift, but it's not quite working the day shift, either, so it completely destroys your day. You get out of work around 2:00 p.m. and it's as though you've awoken after decades of being cryogenically frozen; you're not sure what time it is, what you are supposed to be doing, or who is even around you. Nothing makes sense. And even if you can adapt to starting your after-work life in the middle of everyone else's afternoon, it won't change the brutality of having to deal with people at 5:30 in the morning. If you can, I'd stay away from morning shifts at a coffee shop, as it will only serve to remind you that humanity is often at its cruelest when you are at your most tired.

But I digress.

We're all at different schedules and levels of income, which means that finding a happy medium that pleases everyone when it comes to going out is a battle in and of itself. You're sure to have half your friends talking about how "This shit is so expensive" at literally any establishment you could go to, even if they only drink cans of domestic. The other half is always offering to go to these lavish parties on weekends that are hosted by a magazine, website, or what appears to be a high-class escort service. The fact that these people are often friends may be astonishing, and it's likely they'll stop speaking to each other entirely by thirty, but for now it makes for some tough weekends. The three options—dive bar, club, and house party—seem to each make less sense than the last when it comes to "having fun," but these are our options as they stand.

The House Party: Are We Supposed to Be Sitting Down?

When you're nineteen, a house party is exactly what it sounds like. You're in a structure with four walls, you have no idea who owns it, and everyone is drinking out of red cups. No one brings anything to offer the host, people might steal an iPod, and you can be sure horrendous pictures of you will surface the next morning. There is no shame in walking upstairs into someone's parents' bedroom and having drunk sex with a guy who is studying anthropology and wants to work as a "community organizer." You can just start dancing on the kitchen counter if things are getting boring. You'll meet about a hundred people, twenty of whom you'll add on Facebook the next day, eighty of whom you'll forget forty-six seconds after learning their name. It's a sordid affair, to be sure, but it's quaint in its honesty. "We're here to get drunk. Let's not make this any more complicated than it needs to be."

But as we make it reluctantly into our twenties, the entire idea of a house party and what it should entail becomes increasingly fuzzy. We all have a vague image in our minds about what "adults" do when they gather for an evening among friends, and we all have the same nagging sense that we are, more or less, "adults." We have an inchoate fear that everyone else our age is inviting friends over for a refined evening of witty banter and intellectual debate around a mahogany table in a well-decorated dining room as they sip Chianti and laugh with smug satisfaction. There may even be cigars and brandy in the library, if the conversation turns political. They also probably share tips on how to best manage your railroad empire and clean your monocle. These savvy twentysomethings all know how to make an incredible Beef Wellington and tap-dance out of their kitchen as they serve it, laughing and smiling about how well-adjusted they are and how just incredibly together their shit is.

That is the dinner party of an adult, and, judging by how much of your furniture is still hand-me-down IKEA, you are not yet one yourself. But there is a grating knowledge that the "anything goes"–style Roman orgy that house parties used to be are just not okay anymore. So what do you do when there simply isn't the square footage or kitchen appliances to host a real dinner event? We have these awkward, in-between affairs in which we kind of sit or stand in circles and kind of discuss things as we sip various drinks out of a mix of actual stemware and plastic cups. The topics of conversation and location are rather adult—you all have jobs to discuss and the apartment is at least marginally well-decorated—but you are still not quite grown-ups yet. It sort of feels as if you're a little kid again, scooting around the house in your parents' clothes and shoes. All the elements are there, but nothing quite fits.

Though the party may turn into something halfway decent by the 2:00 a.m. mark, when you've long since switched from Pinot Noir to Jäger shots, the process of getting there involves repeating the question, "So, what do you do?" over and over again, as you awkwardly stand against the kitchen counter. It all has the defeated feeling of the progressive, inevitable slide we're all taking to having dinners with friends that end at a reasonable 11:00 p.m. and are followed by conversations in the sedan on the way home about how nice the brisket was.

You might come across the rare house party among good friends in their twenties that just feels as warm and broken-in as an old pair of jeans, one that doesn't require the pretense of putting out the best snack trays and taking people's coats to prove that you're a big girl now, and those are wonderful, but they become increasingly few and far between. Whether because of geographical distance, or the fact that some of your friends have upped and started getting married/having kids, there are a million reasons why the easy and fun house party starts to dwindle down as you get older. Most of the parties in which the crowd is unfamiliar and the conversation is 80 percent introductions are all going to fall into this same kind of stilted rhythm, leaving the house party a dubious choice at best.

The Dive Bar: I Don't Know
What I Stepped in, But It Was Wet

I'll be honest—I'm not a big fan of the dive bar. I know that for many of you, the idea of someone not liking a place covered with peanut shells and bartenders that scream at you if you don't order clearly enough is nothing short of blasphemy, but bear with me. I'm not as high-maintenance as you might think, and my dislike for dive bars certainly doesn't come from its more-than-fair price points. I don't need to go somewhere fancy to feel as if I'm not accidentally mixing with the paupers. I just find that, in general, the ambience of dive bars is that of "Let's strip this place of any and all charm so that people have no reason to pace themselves when getting completely shitfaced."

From the old guy leering by the jukebox (that will only ever play Springsteen, as if by divine mandate), to the women who crowd the ½-square-inch of bathroom mirror that's not yet covered with graffiti to fix their clown makeup, to every surface being dirty, wet, or some unsettling combination of the two—I just don't like it. Add to this the fact that I consistently feel the need to "dress up" when I go out—for myself more than anyone else—and I'm usually left wearing a cardigan and knee-length dress in the middle of a sweaty dance floor at midnight, and it's just really not my scene.

That being said, I am also profoundly cheap, as are many of my friends. Because of this—our near-allergic aversion to paying more than $5 a cocktail—I often find myself in such environments every single week. And I must say that, in all seriousness, the honesty and affordability of said bars are much appreciated, even if the aesthetic isn't exactly mine. Especially for a group of friends who are, shall we say, diverse on the income spectrum, it presents the best combination of being able to get vomit-y drunk and still not feel as if you're putting anyone out. Provided, of course, that you manage to grab a table early, watch over your belongings like a hawk, and stab your way to the front of the line at the bar/bathrooms, you can have yourself an incredible night.

Unfortunately, though, the entire concept of a dive bar has started to change its form in big cities, notably in cultural hot spots. What was once charming because of the owner's complete lack of care for the upkeep of the establishment has now become a symbol of cool disaffection. It used to be kind of fun reading the various graffiti argue with each other in the bathroom stall as you pitied the girl next to you heaving what was clearly three days' worth of food into her toilet, given that the drinks you would get when you left the bathroom would be a third the price of anywhere else. Now, "cool" bars that strive for some kind of "youthful, carefree"—let's be honest, "hipster"—appeal leave their building in the same state of disarray, but continue to charge $10 for a gin and tonic. The dive bar aesthetic—or rather, its distinct lack of one—has been co-opted and transformed into just another strain of douche.

It's arguable that the faux-dive is the worst choice you can make when hitting the town. It generally turns out to be the worst of all worlds between the outrageous prices, the crowd of twenty-five-year-old guys named Noah who are DJ/graphic designers, and the ambience that, even though this place isn't actually supposed to be cool, you're still not cool enough for it. The faux-dive is the bastion of the false, affected hipster aesthetic and—despite this word being generally overused into meaninglessness—represents all that is terrible about the idea.

While a genuine dive bar is not that hard to find if you really scour a city or a smaller town—and the prices will still be more than reasonable—it's getting to be a much rarer find. Neighborhoods are gentrified into oblivion if you leave them alone for more than ten minutes, and what was once a cool place to get stepped on while you screamed over $2 well drinks is now a place that you still have to walk through an underground cave to get to, but will now be filled with all the people you try to avoid when you're working at the coffee shop.

It seems that the dive bar is a quickly fading option.

The Club/Lounge:
Hey, Girl, Wanna Sit at Our Table?

Has there ever been a double-edged sword quite as sharp as a hot lounge on a Friday night? It's this sort of ethereal place where the people are good-looking, the drinks have sentence-long names, and the lights are ice blue or brothel red—never in between. And yet, despite all its attention to aesthetic and cool, there are few places that make you feel like more of a loser when you're there. At some point when you're in a club—usually when you catch a glimpse of yourself in the austere bathroom mirror in your most painfully conjured-up outfit—you always think to yourself, "What the hell am I doing here? I clearly don't belong here." If you are capable of fully enjoying an evening out at a club without ever once considering what the spiritual and intellectual implications of your coming there were, I don't think we could ever be friends. You must think far too highly of yourself for me to even think about talking to you.

Aside from the fact that the ambience is generally one of sweaty douchebag and his harem, the ability to hold anything resembling a fulfilling conversation is guaranteed to be completely eroded by the throbbing Chris Brown music and the screams of bachelorette parties in the corner doing shots in their crowns made out of dildos. In the best-case scenario, you can hope for a conversation along these lines:

You: Hey, it's really loud in here!

Friend: What??

You: I said, it's really fucking loud in here!

Friend: What? Oh, man, I'm so drunk. What did you say??

You: It's loud.

Friend: Huh?

You: I love you. I don't really know how to say this any other way. I mean, it's something that I have been wanting to tell you for a long time, and I don't want you to feel weird about it, and if you don't reciprocate it I totally understand. But I just love you, and I want you to know that, and I hope you can continue to be my friend even though you know this about me now. I love you.

Friend: What??

You: Shots?

Friend: Shooooots!!!

It's just that every person in a club has to actively put on a persona, an attitude, that justifies the $12 drinks or the $100 bottles of Champagne. You can't just walk into an empty room wearing sweatpants and insist on that kind of markup—you have to be the kind of person who accepts such a scenario. Granted, you could be one of the pop-collared dudebros who have long since become that person full time and actually think there are times in which the club, logisti-

WHAT YOU CAN EXPECT
FROM YOUR DRINK

TYPE OF COCKTAIL	PRICE	LEVEL OF BUZZ	LEVEL OF CLASSINESS	LEVEL OF HANGOVER
Bellini	$$	not very drunk	very classy	little hangover
Jägerbomb	$$	very drunk	not classy	big hangover
Top-shelf Gin martini	$$$	hammered	very classy	little hangover
Cheap Wine	$	somewhat drunk	somewhat classy	big hangover
Long Island Iced Tea	$	hammered	not classy	big hangover
Domestic Beer	$	not very drunk	not classy	little hangover
Apple Martini	$$$	hammered	not very classy	big hangover
Whiskey Neat	$$	hammered	super classy	big hangover

cally speaking, "can't handle them." But you can't save them. They have abandoned reality somewhere along the way, and no longer realize what a circus of absurdity and cologne a club really is.

Even the clubs that are rendered slightly more justifiable by their themed parties, sponsored events, and open bar for ladies are eventually revealed for their inherent skeeziness sometime around the midnight mark. At a certain point, the floor becomes a glorified safari, the women on display like a particularly well-coiffed pack of gazelle, the men in their canvas jackets, pointing and staring before considering whether or not they could poach one before tonight. It is a question of being constantly watched, observed, and judged. Whether coyly glanced at over the rim of a drink, or downright glared at by a jealous dancer on the floor whose shoes are far from being that cute, it's one giant competition.

So we bring our friends, of course, to at least briefly escape the cloying atmosphere of posturing and move-making, but that usually ends in incoherent screaming at each other as you dance in a rough circle in some dark corner. Though it certainly provides a buffer from the rivers and waterfalls of skeezers coming from every conceivable direction, it's certainly not the place to have a coherent conversation or really enjoy each other's company.

Let's be honest: There are only so many times you can scream about how much you love a particular song before the dance floor loses its charm. Not to mention, after a certain point, the entire building takes on the humidity and general odor of a well-used gym sock. It's just not the best place to be if you're looking for a reasonable night out.

So where do we go? What are the options that leave us all happy, wealthy, and relatively dry at the end of the evening? Well, we could all take up hobbies that don't involve drinking but allow us to learn something new while enjoying each other's company for what it is in its natural state—having real conversations unmarred by inebriation or societal pressure to go home with a sex partner. We could all sign up for activities together, take dance lessons or join a bowling league, or even do some volunteering and then maybe cook for each other afterward. If you think about it, it could probably be pretty fun and easy on the pockets.

Just kidding. We'll probably just drink on a rooftop when the weather clears up.

Chapter
5

LOVE AND DATING

Or, How to Appease Your
Mother When She Asks If
You're Seeing Anyone

Do you want to get married? What about one of those wacky fondant-covered cakes with intricate designs on them—do you want one at your wedding? Are you interested in having kids? Would you like a house in an up-and-coming suburban neighborhood with easy access to the city center, but enough space to have a yard for everyone to photogenically play around with your Golden Retriever? Do you dream of a life of blissful monogamy, complete with the professional and social success that always seems to be an unspoken background of all the couples we tend to emulate?

If your answer to any (or, God forbid, all) these things is an enthusiastic "yes," I feel compelled to inform you that navigating the dating scene is going to be a bit of a challenge. I'm not saying that there isn't a Prince (or Princess) Charming out there with good credit and a nearly identical five-year plan to yours. I'm just saying that you're in for kissing a lot of frogs in the meantime.

What's worse, many of these frogs are—aside from not interested in constructing anything resembling a future with their long-term partners—praised and rewarded by society for stringing others along. Things that were once considered requirements in one's mid- to late twenties (a good career, some property, a nice relationship with a view of the future, interests that are only marginally dependent on drinking) are now the stuff of anachronistic losers. You meet a twenty-five-year-old today who has a fiancée, a three-bedroom apartment, a fulfilling job, and a good deal on a new car, the first question is "What is wrong with him?" There has to be some trapdoor, underneath which there lies a dizzying history of mental illness or chopped-up torsos. None of us just "work everything out" in our twenties now, and the expectations that used to keep all of us in a single-file toward the local chapel to tie things up neatly have evaporated into thin air.

It's only fair, considering that so many bright-eyed/bushy-tailed young adults who spend their entire childhood being convinced that a college degree is the infallible key to a life of financial security and social prestige now find themselves holding diplomas that are worth less than the fancy-ass paper on which they're printed. To continue to expect that everyone would want (or be able to logistically support) the 2.5 kids and a dog playing in the well-mortgaged garden would be ridiculous, and leave everyone feeling like even more of a disappointment to their parents than they already do.

Speaking as a woman, I can certainly say that being able to explore my young adult life without the constant, grating questions of "When are you going to fulfill your purpose and start popping out kids to pay for?" is pleasant (though I am under no illusions that my reprieve from baby-making pressure will last forever). And yes, having to grow up with the expectation that I would be fending for myself and not relying on a man to subsidize my life, while initially difficult, undoubtedly results in a life that is far more fulfilling and full of choice.

There are definitely upsides to no longer having to fit into a razor-thin spectrum of what is considered "appropriate social development" in our twenties, but the willy-nilly "No one can get a job, so everyone just do whatever the fuck you want" has its pitfalls. The premium that was once put on a certain amount of maturity and responsibility as we eased into adulthood has been replaced, in many circles, by a strange idolization of whoever appears to give the least amount of fucks.

If you're dating a man and he, at the ripe old age of twenty-six, has yet to secure gainful employment, an apartment not furnished by things he found next to a dumpster, or the ability to return a call within a twenty-four-hour window—that's okay! In fact, if he is hot in that mysterious, greasy-haired way, you've got the pick of the litter! The key, it seems, is to remain as emotionally detached and disengaged from the future as humanly possible, existing in some kind of limbo in which you are old enough to rent a car, yet still eat dry Lucky Charms from the box because you cannot be bothered to buy milk. These traits, once regarded as the stunted adolescence that we were heavily discouraged from falling into ourselves, have now become the markers of someone cool enough to chase after fruitlessly for the bulk of our twenties.

But where everything becomes really complex is not so much in identifying the Forever Teenagers™ as it is in separating them from the people who are working hard but simply have not yet carved an adult path for themselves in this society. While some people are looking to float around aimlessly, break hearts, and linger on someone else's joint every now and again, other people are achieving the same lackluster results in the face of actual effort.

You could end up dating guys who fall all along a continuum in terms of personality and work ethic. I would say they generally fit into one of four categories: Hard-Working Harry; Indie Asshole Irving; Successful Stud Sammy; and Perpetual Student Pete. They may appear the same (though it's doubtful that they dress the same), but they couldn't be more different from one another. Identifying them and separating them is as essential to the Carnival of Horrors that is dating in your twenties as finding the perfect little black dress. But what defines each of these types? What makes them who they are? You'll find minor variations, of course, but it's safe to say that they generally fall within the following descriptions.

HARD-WORKING HARRY

HWH is a good guy. And not in the creepy, misogynistic, neck-bearded Redditor way that believes you owe him exactly 20.5 minutes of sex after he exhibits that he's a decent human being—he's actually a good person. He is, as his name suggests, a hard worker. Even though the economy has somewhat limited his options in terms of gainful employment and put a damper on his five-year plan, he is going to put 100 percent into whatever path he is able to take with his career or his studies.

While on the outside, at least financially, he might appear similar to Indie Asshole Irving (there is a decent chance that both of them could be working in a coffee shop, for example), they are fundamentally different in terms of their outlook on life. Hard-Working Harry would never think he was "above" a hard day's work, no matter what ridiculous uniform he is forced to wear by his shift manager. While he may not be able to shower you with the lifestyle you would like at this very moment, you get the distinct impression that as he phases out of his twenties, his commitment will definitely pay off in life. (Also, he would be a totally amazing dad—you can just tell.)

INDIE ASSHOLE IRVING

Perhaps the opposite of Harry, Indie Asshole Irving has taken our generation's overall difficulties with finding gainful employment or maintaining a responsible living environment and gone unkempt-balls-to-the-wall. You can often find IAI working in some basic yet chill job, such as barista for an independent coffee shop or cashier in a secondhand bookstore.

Irving understands that, because he is good-looking and has Adam Levine scruff and several high-quality torso tattoos, he doesn't need to be a decent person. He is perfectly content to flounder throughout his twenties, doing hallucinogens and leaving mysteriously for two weeks to go to a music festival and flood Facebook with the photographic evidence. Nothing about his life is to be taken seriously, except perhaps his occasional White Man Dreads. Concepts like "building a career," "treating your significant other with love and respect," or "bathing frequently" tend to be mere pipe dreams for Irving, and certainly not something you're going to teach him to understand through your patient, giving love. Best to avoid IAI, if possible.

SUCCESSFUL STUD SAMMY

Sammy is lucky. He managed to find a lucrative job in this economy, and he is pretty aware of the high premium that puts on him socially and romantically. He can usually be found wearing a Paul Smith suit and looking chic at fairly expensive lunches in the business district of his city. He enjoys happy hours with work friends at the more bro-y bars in the neighborhood, and has a very clear-cut plan when it comes to making his professional life all he dreams it could be.

Now, it's hard to say whether Sammy is closer to a Harry or an Irving in terms of his outlook toward other human beings. He could have the soul of an Indie Asshole Irving who, aside from his high marks in engineering or business school that enabled him to land a fancy job as a financial analyst, would be spreading HPV to every cute girl at the coffee shop. However, he could be a genuinely good person whose tireless hard work and natural talents in the STEM fields made him highly employable, even in this economic climate. Unfortunately, that is not always something you can tell from afar. You may have to get to know him to find out for yourself.

PERPETUAL STUDENT PETE

While there is nothing wrong with wanting to expand your horizons academically and learn a few new things about yourself in the process, Perpetual Student Pete has taken the concept of being a "student" to astronomical new heights. Nearing thirty, he is still very much entrenched in academia and the lifestyle that goes with it. Usually he's not involved in anything incredibly time-consuming, such as medical school, as that would prevent him from reaping the full benefits of the lax schedule and relatively low societal pressure. Chances are, you're probably not even going to meet people in med school or their residency, as they only leave their decrepit laboratories and hospitals once every few weeks to sit in the sun so they don't die of vitamin D deficiency (at least, to my understanding).

Pete, however, is generally a student of the liberal arts, perhaps pursuing a doctorate in philosophy or something equally "thoughtful." Despite his potentially thinning hair, he is still very much in the throes of getting the undergrads' panties and drinking heavily while still feeling that everything he says is extremely significant. Also, the inevitable question, "Where the fuck is all this tuition money coming from?" is one best ignored, because the answer is usually more horrifying than you could ever have anticipated.

As you can see, the qualities that separate the different types you may encounter are pretty pronounced, even if they're not always visible at a glance. But if you're looking for a romantic partner, it's essential to value the respect for your fellow human and interest in personal improvement above almost everything else. Even if you're shacking up with a Harry who is putting in doubles at a Starbucks and a Target, if he is working to better himself, create financial independence, and have the dignity of supporting himself—he is worth a thousand of the more preening Sammies. No five-figure Christmas bonus is ever worth being made to feel as if someone is doing you a favor by dating you.

This isn't to say that being an Irving, for example, is necessarily a bad thing. If you are most intrigued by being a free spirit who cares nothing about another person's emotions, that's fine. There's an ass for every seat, as my classy grandfather would say. There are surely many other people who want to share with you your love for white-person dreads and four-hour-long monologues about music that no one has ever heard of. For every guy who insists on changing the song constantly at a party to suit his incredibly esoteric tastes, there is certainly someone out there who swoons at the idea of being told what is cool by someone who rarely answers her text messages. That's fine.

But the problem arises when people who are looking for genuine love start falling for Indie Asshole Irving and those like him. The cold truth of the matter is that society now, more than ever, encourages people to foster their inner selfish seven-year-old. Running around with no plans for the future and a complete disregard for the emotions of others—even others you may occasionally claim to love—is just considered par for the course if you're twentysomething and living in a big city. Even those with a prestigious or lucrative job and the potential to comfortably finance a house or family are not in any way expected to do so (which is fine on an individual level, not so good when you're with someone who strongly desires these things).

It's understandable that someone who has taken the concept of playing hard to get and transformed it into an entire lifestyle—spilling over into the work, social, and romantic sectors—might be the epitome of attractive to someone who's always enjoyed a little cat-and-mouse. Irvings, however, are the land mines of today's romantic landscape for anyone looking to settle down. Identifying and avoiding them are essential to maintaining a semblance of self-esteem.

And self-esteem is the essential thing here, because we can't change what other people are going to do with themselves, and it's not our place to force someone to want the same kind of future we want (as though that were even possible). I think we've all wasted a decent amount of time on an Irving, waiting for the soft, malleable heart of gold that must have certainly been under all those emotional-guy-lyric tattoos to finally show itself and make all our hard work worth it. But that never comes, and it's no one's fault, really. Speaking personally, I recall one evening spent within a block of my then-boyfriend's work as he promised that he would be leaving within the next twenty minutes to go out to an event with me. Two hours later, I come to find that he had been drinking beers with several friends for the past hour and a half with some coworkers/friends and had not even bothered to inform me of his whereabouts. When asked why he hadn't answered my calls, he told me without even an ounce of remorse, "My phone was on silent."

At the time, I was furious with him for having treated me that way and making me, once again, look like such an enormous ass in front of everyone when all I wanted was a bit of his attention. Now, looking back, I am mostly angry with myself for having continued to waste any time on someone who was so clearly not interested in being a decent person. In all seriousness, it's not your job to make anyone else suddenly morph from frog to prince with your magical genitalia. It's by far the best decision to find someone who, right out of the gate, is at least a moderately good person who won't constantly leave you shakily checking your phone like some lovestruck cokehead.

So who do you date? Where do you find him? And how do you know that he is the right person for you? Now that we are no longer in the alcohol-soaked constant socialization-demanding confines of higher education, the opportunities to meet people organically have become increasingly slim, and society has

THE IDEAL GIRLFRIEND AND BOYFRIEND
ACCORDING TO SOCIETY

Pretty with minimal
makeup/effort

Chill demeanor

Large breasts

Sexy lingerie under
modest clothes

Small waist

Kim Kardashian butt

Non-threatening
income

Few if any
political views

Joyful laugh
(at your jokes)

Genuine interest in
nerd-things without
being a nerd girl

Full head of hair

Winning smile

Over six feet

Commanding speaking voice

Just the right amount
of chest hair

Fashionable but not
"trying too hard" outfit

Well-endowed

Diversified stock portfolio

Subscription to *GQ*

Low body fat

more than decided what kinds of qualities are going to get you a gold star in the dating pool. (Of course, desiring and expecting to find any or even most of these qualities in a single person—and magically making them fall in love with you—is every shade of absurd, but dating is nothing if not an efficient way to make us all feel ludicrously inadequate.)

And keeping in mind that the search for this perfect match will include stringently avoiding Irvings, there is not a moment at which your eyes can be too peeled. But there are distinct pros and cons to each location at which you will potentially find a date, and you'll likely have to navigate all of them to finally kiss your Prince(ss) Charming.

Places to Meet Someone Special

WORK

Pros:

- You are in constant proximity with one another, making organizing your time spent together fairly easy.

- There will always be stuff to talk about, even if it is tedious office gossip.

- You get that hot, forbidden, copy-room fondling that undoubtedly fuels the libidos of 70 percent of office romances.

- The air of "Do they or don't they?" floating around your

coworkers makes you temporary celebrities among your team.

• Lunch hours at the taco truck are made infinitely more romantic.

Cons:

• You might have to eventually report this to HR, which will undoubtedly take away some of the "sexy" factor.

• Talking about work is a fairly redundant activity, given that you both experience more or less the same thing every day.

• You are in constant proximity, which, let's be honest, can get kind of grating after a while.

• Should you break up, your entire professional life will get kicked up several notches from "somewhat boring but pretty good, all things considered" to "absolutely unbearable, why do I have to work two cubicles down from someone who was inside me a short two months ago?"

SOCIAL GROUPS

Pros:

• The awkward "Let's integrate one another into our respective friends groups" is not necessary, as you both come from the same primordial friends soup, so to speak.

• Hanging out is easy and convenient to organize.

• You likely know each other fairly intimately, and are therefore less likely to be surprised with things like a tendency to nitpick about irrelevant things, or a burgeoning murder-and-dismemberment hobby.

- The dividing of your social life between your two respective friend groups is a headache you won't have to endure.

- You have fewer people to invite to your wedding, therefore cheaper.

Cons:

- When you break up, literally everyone you know mutually is going to have to endure an awkward "Let's decide who we love more" dance in which they try simultaneously to offend no one and please everyone, resulting in everyone hating each other. Depending on the ugliness of the breakup, this precarious picking sides routine could result in the complete dissolution of some of said friendships.

- Almost every local haunt you enjoy is now going to be forever colored by the memory of your failed relationship.

- You may very likely have to bear witness to your ex now dating yet another in your mutual friends group.

- Social gatherings are guaranteed to be uncomfortable for at least a month, if not much, much longer.

ONLINE DATING

Pros:

- You can hide behind a profile that only presents the most palatable parts of yourself, letting unsuspecting strangers fall in love with you before they get the full picture of that weird thing you do when you laugh and your tendency to send back food on almost every order at a restaurant.

- Highly advanced algorithms are there to reaffirm what you already suspect: The guy with the fedora in his profile picture and *Atlas Shrugged* among his favorite books may not be the perfect match for you.

- You have a catalog of potential mates to choose from at your disposal, making the rejection of someone for rather superficial reasons less of a risk than it would be in real life. (Now you finally don't have to marry someone with a wonky toe simply because she fulfills every other need you have! The future has truly arrived!)

- Your self-esteem is in for a daily boost from a veritable army of suitors who send you unsolicited and ham-handed compliments that you promptly delete with a haughty laugh.

Cons:

- From now on, when you're asked by older, less hip loved ones where you met your partner, you will be forever obligated to mumble under your breath the name of a dating site that you are terribly ashamed to have used.

- You won't have a cute meet-story to regale to your future children.

- The thrill of getting to know someone little by little is somewhat dulled, as you start things off with a pretty expansive knowledge of each other's personal tastes and at least several flattering photos of each other.

- There will always be at least one asshole who judges you for having met the love of your life on a website.

THE BAR

Pros:

- You're drunk, so whatever normal filters you put over yourself to make things nice and presentable for someone you're interested in have been completely numbed. If he falls in love with that version of you, he's ready for anything.

- Chances are high that your cute meet-story may involve dancing to "Thriller" under the sparkling light of the dance floor.

- You know this person knows how to go out and have a good time from the get-go.

- No one makes a pretense about the fact that this place is entirely designed for picking people up to have sex/find romance, making starting the conversation all that much easier.

Cons:

- You met at the bar, which is kind of skeezy.

- People you meet at a bar are generally not the people who you one day see yourself starting a family with. Or, if they are, they are certainly not putting the "Let's get married and take out a mortgage together" foot forward while wobbling toward the bathroom.

- There is a more than decent chance that you will be wasted when you first meet each other, and if someone is really that into Drunk You, do you trust him as a person? I mean, I know Drunk Me, and she is kind of awful.

I've met people in all these situations, and have found assholes and princes in each one. The truth is, we have more ways than ever to put ourselves in proximity with new people and present ourselves in the way we want to. We can be a totally different person on a dating website than we are at a bar, which is also totally different from the person our friends know and (mostly) love. Is this a good thing? Debatable. But it certainly means that the "other fish in the sea" platitude that is so far from comforting when you are covered in snot and mascara, crying over a devastating breakup, is more true than ever. You can organize a week full of dates, one each night, if you are so inclined (and I know more than one person who does that, because why the hell not). The end of a relationship is just that, a brief end to something that could be the beginning of a million new, infinitely better, experiences.

We even have places like Missed Connections pages, where the people who stared at each other for a little longer than would be considered appropriate in the produce aisle of the local grocery store—people who only a few short years ago would have gone the rest of their lives only thinking of each other as "asparagus hottie"—are now able to potentially find each other once more and start what could be a lifelong romance. Technology and people's growing confidence to approach one another have made this possible. It's insane, the degree to which we are all constantly able to connect.

So why do we stay with Irvings when they are clearly terrible, and we could certainly do so much better? When we could go online and, within a twenty-four-hour period, have a dozen new potential Loves of Our Lives who are "matched" to us with some insane percentage like ninety-two. (How is that even possible? That seems absurd.) What is the motivation to settle for something that is definitely not mutually beneficial, or even enjoyable? I find it hard to believe that we have some tiny chip lodged in all our brains that says, when we are blown off for the third evening in a row, "This is marriage material right here. Mate with this. Reproduce with this. Put more of this into the world." I just can't believe we are this self-defeating. But I think there is some truth to the notion that, because we are all having a tough time establishing ourselves and finding a real pathway to success, independence, and fulfillment, it is hard to demand that kind of self-assurance from someone else.

Our mothers would not have considered getting serious with someone at twenty-five who wasn't interested in the long term, who wasn't able, willing, or working toward being able to provide for a family and set up a home somewhere. Those were basics, and the respect that came along with those basics was essential. But today we have no individual pressure to make big decisions (or, at least, no one is surprised when it isn't possible), so we are willing to accept relationships that linger on in the not-so-serious stage for years on end. Years. Literal years.

I know people personally who have moved in with their significant others of several years, with no real plans for the future and no real feeling that their relationship is a priority in the SO's life. When I ask them what they want, they usually respond marriage, kids, a house somewhere, being a real family—pretty standard things. And even though it is clearly not in the cards right now for this couple, my friends are happy to stay and prolong the whole "We're just kind of casually seeing each other" process, moving in unceremoniously solely because it saves money. This is not what they want, but they assume that there is nothing better out there or that it would be unfair to ask for more. Somewhere along the line, the idea that you should only be investing in people who ultimately want the same things as you went completely out the window—likely around the time bath bombs became popular.

But someone doesn't have to be rich or even financially comfortable to be moving toward the goals of one day establishing himself. At the end of the day, the defining factor in whether or not someone is going to be a good match is how he treats you and how he makes you feel about yourself. When you're not a priority for someone else, you can feel it, and there is no reason to actively put yourself through the daily confidence beating that comes from being with someone who is indifferent to your existence. Seriously, it is incredibly humiliating to be clearly more into someone than he is into you. It's the emotional equivalent of walking around all day with a square of toilet paper stuck to your shoe and no one telling you; you just look like a fool, and everyone kind of silently pities you.

We know that we can do better. We know that there are kind Petes, there are empathetic Sammies, and there are legions of underrated Harries. We have options, endless options, and there is no reason not to pursue them. It doesn't matter if we're not going to be in the white-picket-fenced house with 2.5 children and a Shetland Sheepdog by the time we're thirty-one; it just matters that we're moving in that direction and treating each other with respect and love. You can go to the bar and drunkenly tell someone how much you love him within the first ten minutes of meeting him. You can reach out to a friend who has always interested you, but with whom you never really wanted to risk the friend dynamic. You can suck it up and go on OkCupid, and realize that there is only, like, a 3:10 skeezeball ratio overall on that website.

And if you don't want to get married or have kids—or even have a long-term relationship—congratulations, you no longer have to. Whether or not you're going to hit thirty and suddenly throw it into reverse, like a heavily abused rental car, and decide that you do want to start something concrete with someone, it doesn't matter now. We are lucky enough to have been born into time when we are not all universally expected to be impregnating/impregnated by the time we reach twenty-five with no real future outside of living vicariously through our children for the rest of our lives. I think it's easy to forget how amazing it is when someone reminds you, in your twenties, how "young" you are, and how you have "so much time" to be looking for what exactly you want out of life. That is such a huge step forward from pretty much every other point in history.

I admit that I am biased, in that I've known pretty much since I was aware of my surroundings that I one day want to get a ring put on my finger and start spawning, but I have nothing but respect for people who don't want that. And, to be frank, the world is kind of your oyster at this point if you're not wed to the notion of finding something serious. So many people out there right now are just looking to date casually, and are totally open about it. Hell, you can even mosey on over to SeekingArrangement and get yourself a brand-new tacky Lexus while you work on your career or your studies. You have free rein to do so, and innumerable websites with which to locate singles in your area who are looking for a similar ratio of sex–to–actual feelings.

The point is that it's the fucking twenty-first century, and there's no excuse for any of us—no matter what we're looking for—to be stuck in a situation that isn't what we want. We can literally meet people from across the globe who can put in a concise little paragraph under a picture of themselves exactly what they want out of the next few years of their life. If you are making excuses as to why you are waiting it out with someone who will magically morph overnight into something you are actually interested in, you are wasting your time in the most painful way. You are never going to be this sexy, this energetic, this free of responsibility again in your life. Now is the time, if there ever was one, to be experimenting and going on dates and only getting serious when you feel like it—or remaining completely romance-free for a while, if that floats your be-vibrator'd boat. We have Grindr now; we are officially in the future we always dreamed of. There is no reason not to be yourself.

FINANCES

Or, How to Finish the Month
Without Crying into Your Ramen

Few things seem more intimidating to a young adult who has gone through his entire life without having to contemplate money in a concrete sense than the prospect of having to manage an entire budget by himself. Both sides of the equation—from consistently bringing ever-increasing sums of income into your bank account, to keeping the spending at a reasonable and sustainable pace—seem unrealistic to keep up for an entire life. Unfortunately, though, money just seems to become more necessary, more complicated, and more tightly wound up with other people as you get older. The days when your money was entirely yours to do with what you like (which mostly just entailed buying a staggering amount of Fruit Roll-Ups when taken to a grocery store) are gone forever. (Sidenote: I have not bought nearly the amount of soda and cake that I anticipated I would when I had complete control over my own money. Adulthood blows.)

Money management, aside from being a profession relegated to obese men with monocles and pinstriped suits, is just not fun. Strangely enough, no matter what kind of money you're earning, you'll still find a way to spend a disproportionate amount, which leaves you frustrated and/or nervous at the end of the month. As anyone who has gone from an $8-per-hour gig to earning real-ish money (and possibly back again) can attest, there is no amount of money you can earn that will just be "enough" and allow you to live whatever lifestyle you want without having to be concerned about your bills. I mean, technically, you could be a billionaire, but I'm gonna go out on a limb here and guess that twentysomething socialites aren't hanging on every word of my financial advice.

Personally speaking, I have only in recent times come into a certain kind of coherence with money. For most of my life, even when I was being forced by my parents to save my after-school job money, my life's purpose seemed to be to indiscriminately drain my checking account until I was in tears, looking at the teller like an abandoned puppy, as though she were going to be able to do anything about my negative balance and merry-go-round of overdraft fees. I often come across things I purchased in the financial fugue state that was my life between sixteen and twenty-one, and I am overwhelmed with self-loathing. I went through a significant Lilly Pulitzer phase, convinced that buying $300 dresses when I was making minimum-ish wage and was still a student was a positive move for my future. Aside from looking like someone's tragic, WASP-y stepmom who gets white-wine drunk and hates her life (no one should ever wear a pink dress with a mint-green cardigan, and yet, how many times I did just that), I was burning through everything I'd saved with no thought to the moment when I would actually need it.

Despite how much useless information we absorb during K–12 education, we never take a class that is just like, "Hey, shitheads. This is what a checking account looks like. This is what a budget is. This is what taxes are." I would exchange my entire mathematical education for a weeklong workshop on how to set up a 401K.

I'm not going to say that no one tried to instill proper financial protocol in my thick skull—I can hear my parents yelling right now about how all they did was try to convince me that I was wasting my precious, precious savings—but I was just not trying to learn. Perhaps if it were something we all had to learn and had a grade that depended on really comprehending the material, I would have taken it in more. (Though probably not.)

In any case, money is something that most of us kind of have to learn about through trial by fire. Many of us are going to reach a point at which, all of a sudden, we're just like, "Oh, fuck. I have, like, no money. I really need to get my shit together, because I can't be dancing around thirty and still eating bread with a slice of American cheese put in the microwave as two out of my three daily meals." There's no shame in struggling—this is coming from a person who, on more than one occasion, rolled up to the gas station with a wobbly stack of pennies, ready to see exactly how much that could get me. I shook that gas nozzle to the very last drop, eager to get every single millicent's worth of my fuel. We are all going to reach palpable lows in our financial lives that leave us at best, humiliated, at worst, considering selling our internal organs on the Internet. The idea is to work consistently toward clawing your way out of said pits of monetary quicksand, always thinking of what you can do better or spend less on in order to make everyday life less painful. Though it is not always easy to identify where the money is disappearing to, there are some universal things that abscond with our discretionary funds almost universally.

But sometimes everyday life and personal habits can ruthlessly undermine even the most budget-conscious mind. It seems innocuous enough, but transportation can be one of the most efficient ways of burning through unintended amounts of money every month—often while getting nothing tangible in return. There are cars, of course, which are more aptly described as money-burning kilns with wheels attached. There's the actual cost of the car (whether bought outright or paid for over a series of painstakingly expensive months), the insurance, the gas, the maintenance, the repairs, the tolls. Even parking spaces themselves can be a source of never-ending money absorption. I think that, to this day, I owe the city of D.C. about $500 in unpaid parking tickets. (I'm getting to that, you guys, I promise.) But how many times can you circle a block when you are late to pick up something from a dry cleaner before you just kinda go "Fuck it," and park directly in front of a fire hydrant? We think that leaving our hazards on will save us, but, oh, it will not.

Sure, we could take public transportation—and we often do—but how feasible is that in many midsize cities that, for some reason, have decided that giving their citizens an affordable, efficient, environmentally friendly way to move around would be nowhere near the top of their priority list? And even if you do get your monthly bus or metro pass, what do you do after a long night of imbibing sweet liqueurs, when all your transport options have been exhausted? You do what many of us do: You take a taxi. (Can we just officially rename the act of "taking a cab" as "taking a $20 bill out of your pocket and burning it as you cackle maniacally"?) When I think of all the money I have lost to unnecessary cab rides, my entire being shudders with the cold, drifting winds of my exhausted checking account.

Transport is but one lowly example of the kind of blockades that are set up throughout a young adult's life to prevent him from living in financial equilibrium. It seems that everywhere you go, there is a new thing to do or a new way to do it, something that everyone is doing that you now need to be doing as well. You face unintended expenses, rising rents, and friends who are all going out, and you run the risk of looking like a cheap jackass if you do not join them.

THE WAYS WE WASTE OUR MONEY

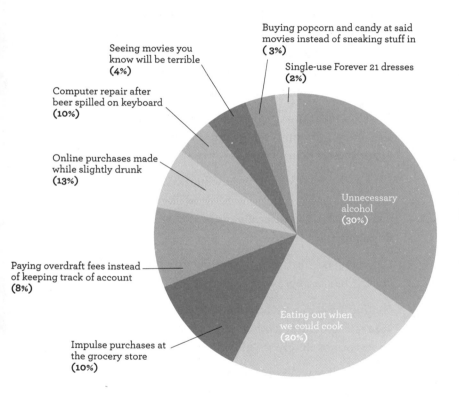

Buying popcorn and candy at said movies instead of sneaking stuff in
(3%)

Single-use Forever 21 dresses
(2%)

Seeing movies you know will be terrible
(4%)

Computer repair after beer spilled on keyboard
(10%)

Online purchases made while slightly drunk
(13%)

Paying overdraft fees instead of keeping track of account
(8%)

Impulse purchases at the grocery store
(10%)

Unnecessary alcohol
(30%)

Eating out when we could cook
(20%)

The Unexpected Expenses of Being an Adult

- Having to attend multiple birthday parties for friends that are held in places like restaurants and bars, where the food and drink are devastatingly far from being free. (Unlike a regular night out, a birthday night is one that you can't just delicately decline and pretend as if nothing happened.)

- The aforementioned taxis to and from almost every event that either requires crippling "going out" shoes or ends at an unreasonable hour.

- Offering a round for everyone while you're out, which you can by no means afford, but which seems like a good idea when you are in the "I am literally made of $100 bills" stage of your drunkenness.

- Delivery food when you can't motivate yourself to look like enough of a human being to go outside.

- Getting a real meal at lunch during work, instead of packing yourself something both nutritious and affordable, as you know you absolutely should be doing.

- Realizing that you are now, as an adult, required to get everyone gifts at holidays, instead of just receiving them like some childish vacuum of materialism. (This is also often the moment where you realize that Christmas is less fun when you're paying for a significant part of it.)

- Travel to go see people who have magically migrated out of your life/geographical region upon graduation.

- Weddings. (Ugh, weddings.)

- Random shopping purchases that you make because you either want to cheer yourself up or crumple entirely under the steely gaze of an overly aggressive salesgirl.

- Purchases that, while not so random, are way beyond your means. There is a difference here between buying a $10 shirt at H&M and buying the exact same shirt in form and function for $300 because you think it looks cool. (Spoiler alert: It never looks *that* cool.)

- Rent which, by being in an incredibly expensive city that you "have" to live in because it is the "best city ever," basically beats your checking account into an unrecognizable pulp once a month.

- Keeping up, in one way or another, with friends who are very far away from your financial lane—whether as a result of their own successes or parental subsidies.

- Diet/exercise/fitness products that you will use/eat/try about three times before promptly abandoning them, regardless of cost.

- Beauty/skin/hair care products that only get more complex and expensive every year.

And these are just some of the more egregious offenders. The truth is that a huge number of the expenses of our daily lives are nothing more than that: innocuous, everyday things. We simply never imagined that we would have to buy them. Few things can quite re-create the sinking, slowly forming depression brought on by realizing that you have to buy things like toilet paper and soap, regularly, all by yourself, for the rest of your life. Things like this always seemed like constants, like something that would just appear in your cabinets—or, at the very least, not cost so much. But they are incredibly expensive, and often have to be organized into a system of importance in which they fall toward the top when the end of the month comes around. Because no matter how many times we insist that we are spending less this time, until we make a firm budget and stick to it, getting through the month with a decent amount of savings and no stomach-churning "How am I going to eat?" feelings is not a possibility.

Real budgets, however, have always seemed like the stuff of adults much older than we'd ever imagined ourselves being. People with children, and mortgages, and spouses, and subscriptions to cheese-of-the-month clubs—those are the kinds of citizens who keep their monthly spending neatly organized in an Excel spreadsheet. But there will come a point, without exception, when you realize that you need to have one of these budget things for yourself. This may be difficult to admit, because it implies not only that you are now in an age bracket that is entirely responsible for its own financial future, but also that you have become boring enough to take it seriously.

When you're twenty, there is only "money," and that exists in a kind of nebulous pile in the back of your mind. Much of it is fake, school loan money that you know will one day have to be repaid, but can't imagine actually dealing with. And there are, of course, your parents, who are usually there to help you to some degree. While we all have our varying combinations of "disposable income" and "personal responsibility," rarely do we think in the long term. You have money, and then you don't. It's not a matter of "making it work for you," because how could it? When you're busy taking out as much of it as bank officers will hand you in between cleaning their bifocals, how can you pretend that you are taking the reins of your future firmly in your semiadult grip?

In the interest of full disclosure, I got off quite lightly on the whole student loan front. I have my debts that I'm grudgingly paying off, to be sure (including, but not limited to, the extremely misguided Visa I procured at the ripe age of eighteen and proceeded to max out in a matter of days), but I have it pretty good compared to many of my peers. Many among us are looking at debt that is in the upper five figures, if not more. And while there is no shame in struggling with the unfortunate decisions of our freshly-accepted-to-our-dream-school selves, it certainly makes the whole situation exponentially more difficult.

So how do you make a budget? Speaking as someone who has

only very recently created a somewhat coherent monthly schedule of income and expenses that includes actual bill paying and
not simply dodging phone calls, as well as putting things aside for
a future that may include one day owning something instead of
just renting it for an extended period, I feel on shaky ground at
best to offer a foolproof plan. But from frustrating experience, I
know that certain things do not work. You can shoot yourself in the
foot, as with some of the purchases previously listed, but there are
also more insidious ways of sabotaging what would otherwise be a
healthy relationship between money taken in and money put out.

Don't avoid looking at your bank or credit card statement. It may
be tempting, I know, not to check the damage after a particularly
fruitful night out or a bout of bill paying that leaves you feeling at
once relieved and depressed, but you have to. Aside from the possibility of your card (or card number) having been stolen in one of
your less lucid moments and your remaining blissfully unaware of
the new purchases, it is always important to know the particulars of
your financial status. The difference between going for the luxuri-
ous chicken pesto wrap at your local organic deli and picking up a
cup of ramen from the corner store could be a few dollars that you
only imagine you have. Sure, it does mean encountering those
stomach-dropping moments of "Oh, my god, where the fuck did all
my money go?" on a more regular basis, but it will avoid a bigger,
more long-term disappointment when you finally hold your eye-
lids open and force yourself to look at your bank statement.

Don't make big purchases without planning for them. Coming

from someone who once bought an IKEA couch while in a drunken stupor, staring at my half-broken futon that I hated so much I could not go another day without replacing it, planning is key. Whether it's a coat you've been eyeing forever, a new piece of furniture, or just a plane ticket that is so frustrating—come on, you're just sitting in a flying tube for a few hours, why is it so expensive???—you need to do some serious preparation. Even if you're the cool, spontaneous type who just likes doing things when the spirit moves you, including getting a new washing machine for your apartment, wouldn't you want to get it on sale? That's the thing about taking your time: So often you find that you could buy something you wanted for less money or that you don't need it at all. It's like waiting a minute and thinking about whether or not you really need those Mentos at the cash register, except the Mentos cost $500, and you don't even have that in your savings account right now.

Don't accrue overdraft fees. Motherfucking overdraft fees. My archnemesis, right after shower stall scum and when someone puts an empty bottle of milk back into the refrigerator—overdraft fees. What evil wizard concocted this ingenious plan, allowing unsuspecting bank patrons to spend all this extra pretend Monopoly money that they don't actually have in their accounts, problem-free, until they have to pay it back with added bonus insane charges on top of it that are not even remotely proportional to the purchase itself? You bought a pack of gum that puts you over your limit by sixty-seven cents? Congratulations, you get to pay

$35 for the privilege of not having that embarrassing "Your card has been declined" moment at the gas station cash register. Thank you, bank, for providing my worthless life with this incredibly useful service that doesn't at all ravage my already paltry bank account into a withered husk of its former self.

Don't compare what you have to others. This is simply a game that cannot be won. Whether or not you feel comfortable in your current financial bracket, there is always going to be someone who is better-off than you, has more access than you, seems to be more successful than you, or is capable of doing things you cannot. This is just a fact of life, and it's not going to change because you've figured out your flashy acquaintance's salary down to a $5,000 range by looking up his job online. Chances are that he is, indeed, making much more money than you are. Does this mean that he is happier? Maybe, maybe not. But it's not as though your obsessing over not measuring up is going to suddenly make your boss burst into your office one day and announce via megaphone that you are getting a brand-new salary of $500K a year, plus signing bonus, effective immediately.

Don't stray from your financial lane. If you can afford something, awesome for you. You should integrate said thing properly into your budget and then buy the shit out of it. But if you cannot afford this item or trip or night out at the club, pretending you can afford it to hang out with certain people or give a certain appearance is never a good move. Where do you think all this imaginary money is going to come from? It's either getting sucked directly out of your bank account, where it would have otherwise been used for such necessities as paying bills and eating, or it's going to be put on a credit card. The last thing any of us needs right now is accruing credit card debt over buying a $500 jacket or an entire bottle of champagne at a table in a nightclub. Sure, it's always uncomfortable to have to be like, "No thanks, friends, I would love to join in with this, but alas, I cannot afford it." But no way is that more uncomfortable than realizing you have to subsist on cardboard boxes for the last three days of the month.

There are clearly things to avoid, things that are obvious red flags away from which we need to steer our respective piles of money. But a budget is so much more than just *not* doing certain things; you also have to tackle the whole constructing-an-actual-plan-of-some-kind-for-your-everyday-and-long-term-spending that has to go along with it, which is often more difficult. And the foundation on which to base our budgets often ends up being however much money we are able to get out of our jobs. With many of us still languishing in exploitative, unpaid internships, though, how do we command a salary? How do we determine what we are worth?

Speaking as someone who has pretty much never negotiated for payment—except once when I meekly suggested a fraction more to cover transportation costs and promptly apologized for asking when I was given a firm "No"—I know it's hard. But how else are you going to develop a budget if you don't have a place to start? And the truth here is that you just have to demand a certain amount for yourself. If you are in your twenties, no matter how glamorous or desirable the industry, you cannot allow your youth to be sucked out of you through a crazy straw in some glamorized intern position. While supplementing your hours waiting tables, or babysitting, or even taking a job in a less sexy field is never anyone's first choice when drawing What I Want to Be pictures when we're five, sometimes it's just necessary. After all, if you're living in one of the most expensive cities in the Western Hemisphere, it's better to be managing your professional expectations than to be sharing a studio apartment with four smelly graduate students who steal your leftovers out of the fridge.

Let's say, for example, you are living in New York City and making $25,000 a year, after taxes. To many people fresh out of school, and used to being exploited in unpaid internships instead of presented with an actual chance at income, $25K seems like a decent amount. It's not a lot, of course, but it's a real salary given in compensation for your work—which is more than many of us can say. And it comes with health benefits, which is something most of us never considered a possibility just a few short years before. But with anything beyond a cursory glance, we can see just how "not that much" $25K is. (In the interest of full disclosure, at the time of writing this, I have never lived in New York City. I lived in Paris for some time, though, which is fairly comparable in terms of city expenses napalming your wallet at regular intervals. I would use Paris as an example for this scenario, but I simply can't bear being that twee when I'm trying to be serious about money. Just assume I spend all my money on baguettes that I put in the basket of my vintage bicycle.)

So you make about $25K, and you are twenty-three years old. You are far from being too proud to take a roommate (or several) to reduce living costs, but you are still holding out hope that your room will have enough space to put more than just a twin mattress in, and you would like it if it weren't located somewhere between New Jersey and the moon. So you look around on Craigslist and other fruitful online locales filled with other eager twentysomethings trying to beat each other to death for a chance at a well-placed apartment with a laundry room in the building, and you find a fair number of listings that seem to more or less suit your needs.

After an arduous period of being disappointed, frustrated, and intermittently overjoyed during your search, you find something that is right for you and hasn't already been pounced on by a pack of rabid real estate hyenas. In all likelihood, you probably got a room somewhere in the less-organic market-filled areas of Brooklyn, and you're paying around $800 a month. I'm being generous here—you're probably paying more—but let's be reasonable. Out of the roughly $2,000 you're taking home every month, you've already lost almost half.

It is safe to assume that you'll probably have at least $200 in other bills per month (and again, that is being generous, as there is a more than decent chance that you have student loans, which frequently eat through your pockets like methed-out fabric moths). So now we're down to $1,000 per month after your pre-debited necessities are out of the way. Then we have transportation, around $150 a month (including the errant taxi you'll end up convincing yourself you need to take). After you take out food at about $600 a month (it would probably be less if you didn't go out to Chipotle for so many midafternoon meals, but come on, you know you do), you are left with a fairly paltry sum of $250 a month.

Now, $250 seems like a lot, still. I mean, it's your play money in this scenario, you can do whatever the fuck you want with it, right? Not so. See, as I've recently come to understand, a sizable chunk of that money is going to have to go into the rarely viewed bank account covered in cobwebs and dust labeled "savings," to build something resembling a "nest egg." You are supposed to have this money to fall back on should you need it, to make more long-term purchases, or to put in some fancy-people investment and "make your money work for you." (I'm not sure what this means, precisely, only that fat Republican rich dudes my dad knows have always encouraged me to do this.) Let's say you put $50 a month into savings, and that's a fairly low estimate, as we should theoretically be trying to save much more, if possible.

Two hundred dollars—that's what's left. That should be enough to get anyone through a month of personal expenses and pleasure spending. Thinking logically, we could divide that $200 up a million different ways to allow ourselves both our occasional splurges and a feeling of overall responsibility. But I think we all know that $200 for an entire month's worth of excursions and "just for fun" purchases is a shockingly spendable number, particularly when we account for how much we like to spend after a few cocktails. (It is a well-documented fact that money literally morphs into Monopoly money after the consumption of more than four glasses of wine. You could be on the brink of financial ruin and still insist on paying for everyone's planned additions on their houses if the evening is going well enough.)

If you are prone to making impulse purchases, or engaging in "retail therapy" to repair deep, emotional wounds in your psyche, $200 is nothing. If you live in a city where a "reasonable" price for a cocktail is around $10 and all your friends have a profound fondness for going out and buying as many of them as the bar will sell them in good conscience, $200 is nothing. If you like doing things such as going out to brunch on Sundays, going on semifrequent trips out of state, or wearing clothes that did not, only a few moments before, fall off the back of a truck, $200 is nothing. It's an incredibly easy sum of money to spend, and we only think that it is a lot when we deny just how much of life (from hanging out with our significant others to keeping up with the latest pop culture) is absurdly expensive. The truth is that if you're juggling only a few hundred dollars of spending money every month, many things are going to have to be cut out in order to build any kind of financial foundation.

No matter how much we earn, though, we will always find a way to spend an amount that is proportionally detrimental enough to make the end of the month more difficult than necessary. And, whether we like it or not, planning for the future is about the only way to make sure that we won't find ourselves at some undetermined point down the road with tears in our eyes, comically holding up a stack of red notices from collection agencies as oversized question marks bob over our frazzled heads. Having a decent amount of money to fall back on should you lose your job, or to put toward a retirement that doesn't have to be delayed until you are wheezing feebly at death's door is simply good sense. That means that all of us—yes, even you—need to make a decisive list of everything we spend money on in a month, as well as our long-term financial and professional goals, and start hacking away at that shit with a Weedwacker.

There are things in our daily lives that we can go without, or corners we can cut to make spending a more responsible affair, but it has to start with honesty. As someone who lived most of her life to this point in a state of willful financial ignorance, who is only now sifting through the pile of absurdly unnecessary debts and misguided purchases to forge a path of sustainability,

I can tell you that this is not fun. It is never fun to have to look at what you're doing with the keen, ruthless eye of a True Adult and strike off all the things that you could do without. But, ultimately, to pay bills on time feels good. To have extra money in the bank feels good. To have serious prospects for the future and a plan that enables you to go after the things you want without feeling stretched to your financial limits feels good. And we deserve to feel this way because even though it sucks in the short term, there is something really satisfying about knowing that you have things under control.

So make those difficult choices. Cut out those brunches. Say "no" to those ridiculous nights in those overpriced clubs that make you feel like not even a thousand scalding showers will wipe the smell of douchebag cologne off you and feel better about all the money you saved. While not everything has to go, and certainly not all the time, we can always make conscious choices to stop the hemorrhaging of money that living in a big city in our twenties is all about. Think of all the small steps you can take each day so that you can start hitting the more "significant" milestones in your life—such as partnering up for life, buying a house, making investments, or maybe even spawning—with the kind of serene assuredness that only someone who has been making positive financial decisions for some time now can do. You owe it to yourself to be one of those classy fuckers, treating yourself to a bottle of Champagne every now and again because you are responsible the rest of the time—and I want to see us all get there together.

Chapter
7

FRIENDSHIP

Or, How to Find
Cool People Who
Aren't the Same
Five Coworkers

The first time one of your friends announces her Big Grown-Up Life Change is something you will remember for the rest of your life. Outside of the occasional high school acquaintance getting knocked up/hitched at the ripe old age of eighteen, the moment where you realize that you're all growing up is almost guaranteed to come in your early twenties. Whether it's someone announcing her upcoming nuptials at an age where it is just barely considered legitimate, changing her Facebook profile picture to an unexpected image of a fetus on an ultrasound, or moving into the world of real estate, it's going to come. And no matter what you do, no matter how much you think you may have grown up as a person yourself, you will not be prepared for it.

When I got my first "Oh, shit, my friends are changing" wake-up call, I was in a local dive bar at happy hour, enjoying my freshly minted twenty-one-year-old status by indulging in a Stoli blueberry and soda (which I perceived then, and in many ways still do, to be the Rolls-Royce of the call drink world). One of my friends announced, a little too casually for my liking, that he was in the final stages of purchasing a house with another friend. As I was just barely able to drink and still very much in the throes of "What the hell am I going to do with my life when I actually have responsibilities outside of not spending too much school money on alcohol?," the whole thing seemed like some kind of elaborate joke. How could two people, one of whom I had "dated" when I was twelve years old, be in the process of purchasing something as demanding (and expensive) as a house?

Suddenly, there was a palpable divide between us, one that I didn't quite know how to define at the time. I would later come to understand, having lived through many announcements of this nature, that every time someone makes a big life decision that puts her firmly on one side or the other of "adulthood divide," it creates an automatic tension in the friendship, regardless of intent. The fact is that people are moving on, whether or not you are ready for it yourself. And this house my friends purchased, as with so many life-changing moments still to come, was happening whether I liked it or not. It didn't seem realistic, and yet there it was, in all its fixer-upper glory, ready for the tireless attention of two eager young bros who were now going to be listed as "spouses" on half of their junk mail. (Full disclosure: I ended up living there for the better part of a year.)

In any case, once the floodgates have been opened on the idea that the friends you grew up/studied with are aging into new, more complex phases of their lives, there is no going back. The next few years will be replete with engagement photo shoots, pregnancy announcements, and moves into condos in more family-friendly neighborhoods throughout the city (and even the suburbs). People are going to move around (and you likely will as well), and the once-ironclad dynamics of your social circles will be called into question on every front. With some people moving onto bigger and better things (and not showing even a remote interest in keeping in touch with their roots), and others hanging back in a kind of stunted adolescence you don't want to get dragged into, you're left with a fairly sparse smattering of original friends by the time you all start establishing yourselves out in the real world. When you find yourself on the other side of graduation, several moves, and having to make some of these Big Grown-Up Life Changes yourself, reestablishing a social group in which you feel comfortable is one of the more difficult, yet essential, challenges ahead of you.

As with many things, making and keeping friends is much easier throughout your school years. Aside from being in constant, forced contact with one another and not having too much in the way of responsibility, there is an undeniable air of adventure in everything you do. As you go from grade school to college, you always encounter different, exciting obstacles to overcome and new experiences to undertake, and you're all facing them together. The intellectual and social development that is imposed on us from birth to our early twenties is only navigable when surrounded by awesome people who are having just as difficult a time as we are. (It doesn't hurt, of course, that you have a regular schedule of partying and irresponsibility to act as the cement between your budding bromances.) There is only one time in your life when a bunch of your closest friends are all going to get together and get drunk, run through a suburban neighborhood and draw dicks all over political lawn signs, and that time does not come after the age of nineteen.

We tend to trick ourselves into thinking that these relationships are meant to last forever. Because school-based relationships fly so fast and free (and can go from a midparty introduction to a mushroom-induced philosophical all-nighter in a matter of days), they seem to have a kind of rare charm. Yet even the most free-spirited friend is liable to get a Boston Terrier and move into a one-bedroom with her boyfriend at some point, only seeing you at the occasional brunch, which is spent mostly talking about your respective jobs. One after the other, these people are going to start splintering off, going their own ways and generally making the best decisions for themselves, which do not factor in the pinky-swears to "keep in touch" that they may have made with you at some point. While you are certainly going to keep a few select friends throughout your twenties and beyond, it would be irrational to expect the majority of them to stick around.

Few things, it should be said, speed up this process more palpably than moving away yourself. If, after you finish school, a faraway city (or even country) is your destination of choice, get ready to learn with shocking swiftness that about 80 percent of your "friends" would be more aptly described as "party acquaintances with whom you spent a lot of time because you both liked smoking weed and lived within two miles of each other." The rate at which people will drop out of your life if you choose to move away is sad at first, and then makes a somber kind of sense. Yes, it's kind of sad to realize that the investment of a Skype session every now and again is too much for most of the people you'd once considered very close, but how many friends does one person really need? You'll be making new ones in your new city anyway, and it wouldn't hurt to update your definition of *friend* to "someone who cares about me even on the rare occasion that it is not perfectly convenient for her."

While you're often tempted to go to Herculean lengths to maintain some of your long-distance friends whom you once really loved, it can be pretty pathetic in its returns on investment. If you are becoming the person who makes constant, unmistakable overtures to bond with an old friend—whether through prolonged phone calls or attempts to meet up in one of your cities—and aren't getting too much in response, it's time to call it what it is: friendship masochism. The truth is that some of these people, no matter how much you may have adored them when proximity wasn't an issue, are just not going to stand the test of time or distance. Keeping close with them, if that proves to be depressingly one-sided, is only allowing yourself to get caught up in the scraggly cobwebs clinging to you from the city and social pool you initially tried to leave.

No matter how you end up fracturing off from the warm cocoon of your original social group, though, it's safe to say that you will find yourself as a young adult at the beginning of a life with no real clue as to how to make new friends. It's isolating and somewhat terrifying to realize that if you don't play your social interaction cards right, you could end up becoming a recluse who only leaves her apartment on the rare occasion that she needs to restock the Fancy Feast. Acknowledging that you need to get out there and start carving out your own adult friendships is scary, but necessary. (If you think that this is sad, consider the alternative: You've stayed exactly where you have lived for all or most of your life, and remain closely intertwined with the exact same group of friends you've had for years and years, never exploring life beyond the tristate area or dating options that don't involve people who have already slept with half of your incestuous social group. Is this really preferable? No. The answer to that question is no.)

So where do you find a friend? What is a friend? How do you friend? Up until your early twenties, friendships were something that just happened naturally. You kind of met people, and suddenly there were a million and one circumstances in which you kept happening to see them, and always an opportunity to make things easier on everyone by adding drinking or costume parties into the mix. Nothing was defined too clearly, there was little pressure, and you didn't even have to arrange the times you saw each other. Something was going on all the time that you could attend or get involved in. You never needed a process of having to initiate repeated, prolonged contact. Now, think about it: You literally have to ask someone out on a friend date. You need to work through an entire process to go from meeting a total stranger in some adult context like work, public transportation, or masquerade orgy to making that person someone you could invite to your wedding some day—and the process must be followed fairly strictly so you avoid looking like a giant creeper. The steps to attaining adult friendship, at least in my humble experience, are as follows:

1. Meet a new person in a nonthreatening but still legitimate setting, such as happy hour, a meet-up group, or work.

2. Begin a conversation with her over something benign and universal, such as a mutual project you may be working on, your dislike of the music that is currently playing, or your disapproval of that woman over there's choice to wear leggings as pants.

3. Have a discussion that incites within you an overwhelming feeling of OMG we are fucking soul mates, I bet she hates Keira Knightley just as much as I do.

4. Not know what to do with yourself because this isn't like trying to pick up someone in a bar for the ostensible purpose of going out on a date/having sex, which has an established protocol.

5. Be unsure as to whether or not it would be weird to propose hanging out.

6. Feel as though you might want to clarify that this isn't a

sexual thing, that you just kind of want to become super good friends with her because she's awesome.

7. Clarify that there's nothing wrong with wanting to date her, and if you were interested in her gender, you would totally be down to asking her out, and you're not a bigot or anything.

8. Realize that you may be overthinking this, and you probably don't need to clarify that your interests are purely platonic in the first place.

9. Continue the discussion and become, as the minutes pass, all the more convinced that you two are totally meant to be friends.

10. Muster up the courage and quell the small voice within you that is whispering about how much of a weirdo you must come across as.

11. Ask if she wants to hang out sometime. (This step is made infinitely easier if you are both a bit lubricated socially, and have had enough drinks to be in that phase where everyone you meet is your new potential best friend. If that's the case, both of you will promptly tell each other how wonderful the other one is, how excited you are to hang out, and how honored you would be if she would be the godparent to your firstborn child.)

12. Get a tepid-to-excited agreement to your offer to hang out.

13. Actually hang out.

14. Start working her into your schedule; depending on her involvement in your life (such as a coworker or neighbor), this may either be extremely easy or nearly impossible. The number of adult friendships that have been rendered unfeasible through conflicting schedules is incalculable but undoubtedly very high.

15. Potentially start a new and wonderful friend-romance with your friend-partner found in the tense throes of adulthood.

The thing about developing friendships as an adult, though, is how awkward the first steps of solidifying the bond can be (even after you've jumped the first hurdle of opening conversation with a complete stranger). No one really warns you that, when you're outside the social beginner mode, which is being in constant proximity with people your own age who share many of your more obscure interests, developing an emotional connection with someone is a difficult process. Much as with starting a romantic relationship, it is something that has to be eased into (tee-hee) and treated with a kind of cautious respect, lest you seem like a crazy, friend-starved hyena who has latched onto his emotional femur and begun gnawing away with impunity.

There is a delicate balance to be struck, one in which you are neither too invested in his attention, nor infuriatingly flaky about following up with things. The idea is that you are now a responsible grown-up who is capable of being emotionally forthright and reliable, and yet no one likes the feeling of being friends with a walking day planner who wants to rush into the "close enough to expect frequent calls" stage of things. And unless you work with each other, the chances of things just evolving naturally are slim to none. You aren't seeing each other all the time, you don't have a ton of mutual people to discuss and dislike together, and your day-to-day activities are likely unrelated. (Hell, even your incomes are probably pretty disparate, which in adulthood may be as strenuous on a friendship as having sex with someone's sibling.) If you are meeting people just while you're "out," the "keeping things up" process is going to be an uphill struggle.

And yet, even when a friendship manifests perfectly, those around you will often still have trouble accepting that adult BFF-dom can start in the most unexpected of places. Speaking personally, I once made a very good friend while out in a bar. She happened to be on a date that was going particularly sour, and being that I am a selfless person with a soul and a moral compass that can only be compared to those of Jesus Christ himself, I swooped in and gave her someone to talk to outside of the socially obtuse and rather lecherous man who was foisting himself upon her at every turn. I am fully aware that this puts me firmly in the running for Greatest Cockblock in Human History, but I feel I did the right thing, given the circumstances. In any case, before the night was through, we had talked at length over drinks and exchanged numbers, only to end up becoming very good friends. For us, the process seemed as natural as it was serendipitous. Sure, you don't go out to bars cruising for friends every day, but when it happens, it's certainly a nice surprise.

But many of our friends remarked on how strange it was that we met *just like that*. They expressed a vague fascination with our ability to strike up a friendship with a total stranger with whom we had, at least at first, nothing concrete in common. It seems like the kind of thing that happens in movies, perhaps, where everyone is attractive and charismatic and full of interesting quips about any situation, but not in real life. To us, our friendship was a pleasant bonus on an otherwise average night out. To many around us, it was a vague yet palpable admission of something more sinister. (Most of the more judgmental people are likely assuming that we met on some message board for people who have some horrifying fetish, and, frankly, I'll let their minds wander.)

Whether we realize it or not, though, almost immediately after finishing our schooling (and the cocoon of forced interaction that goes along with it) we become fairly closed-minded about what a friend group is supposed to consist of. Aside from the idea that there are a finite amount of sources from which to draw your meaningful relationships, there is also a definite caste system that begins forming around you, outside of which you are not really meant to socialize. What kind of job you have, how old you are, what kind of money you're making, what part of the city you live in—they are all invisible checkmarks down a list that hovers above all our heads, telling us exactly the kind of people we are expected to be hanging out with.

And even if you are the kind of person who doesn't allow these things to influence your decision making when it comes to potential buddies, that doesn't mean that everyone else isn't going to be making these subtle judgments. You only have to stray several standard deviations away from your professional and lifestyle lane to realize how strict everyone else's social code may be. If you are working a prestigious, high-pressure job, making a good amount of money, chances are you aren't going to maintain your friendship with the guy who works at the coffee shop and uses his spare money to buy fancy whiskey and new Moleskines for his tone poems. While it can sometimes be based in practical things—such as people who work in food service having nearly opposite hours to those who work office jobs—a huge part of it stems from people putting themselves into small niches of society and believing, on some level, that leaving that niche would constitute a kind of betrayal. We can recognize that it's stupid and petty, and yet so many of us end up participating in it without even realizing what we're doing.

Of course, there will always be the good friends from our past with whom we remain in close contact—but that takes just as much effort, if not more so, than meeting new people while out and about in our adult lives. If you're not willing to put in the time for regular Skype sessions, to make treks to their important events, and/or just to visit them from time to time, or to keep up with what they're doing in life with genuine interest and care, they are not going to magically stay in your life forever. We all know the friends who, despite being awesome parts of our life at one point, made absolutely zero effort to continue being there for all of life's changes and events and thus sort of faded into nothingness. If you want to be able to overcome the naturally different directions you're being pulled in by life choices, geographic location, and social status, you're going to have to make it work yourself.

As your prospects get narrower and narrower, it seems only natural that you break out of the more confining aspects of social interaction that adulthood brings. Who cares if you and your closest friends vary in age or income? Why aren't things such as worldview, sense of humor, or personal principles more important factors when it comes to deciding who we want to hang out with this weekend? When we are in school, the people we choose to spend our time with have earned it through being genuinely cool people. As we get older, though—and age into a bracket where we have literally zero limits on the kinds of people we could be meeting if we put a little effort into it—the chances of being foisted into the same boring group that we don't really like just because they are similar to us on paper are staggeringly high. In fact, there are only a few groups of people you are likely to move around in, if you don't take matters into your own hands.

Work Friends

These are the people you see day in, day out, and most likely there is nothing wrong with them. Even though you are encouraged, through the relentless machinery of capitalism, to compete against them for your very life, they are probably pretty cool. Depending on how dedicated to your job you are, and/or how many hours you're putting in, they could end up being your central social group entirely by default. Many times you get sucked into a routine of hanging out almost exclusively with work people simply because you have neither the time nor the energy to set things up with people who aren't walking out of the building with you at that very moment. As an added bonus, you have nearly endless things in common with them, even if that means that a huge number of your conversations will end up centering around work, which is ostensibly the thing you're trying to avoid by socializing in the first place. Overall, work friends will likely form a kind of baseline to your daily life. They may not be the people you would pick if you had a choice, but they are decent and readily available. I like to think of them as the Subway sandwich shops of friend circles.

It should be mentioned, though, that there is still a veneer of professionalism that coats all these interactions. While letting loose and having fun is a given in any friendship, there will always be a certain degree to which you must hide yourself, lest you be branded as the insane, prone-to-crying lush you sometimes are on more spirited nights out. The last thing anyone wants is the boss to casually find out about your true feelings for him when you accidentally let it slip at a work happy hour the night before. Also, if you add your work friends on Facebook, they will know when you're lying about being sick because you are brutally hungover.

Old Friends

These are the remnants of your social group from when you were but a naive young sprite with your whole life ahead of you, not yet crushed by the prospect of having to center your otherwise sweet life around a nine-to-five job. Likely acquired while in adolescence, college, or even childhood, these are the people you've known "forever" and with whom, through a decent amount of geographic luck, you've been able to remain in close contact. Because of your shared history, you automatically feel a depth in your interactions, even if you weren't incredibly close when you initially became friends. Because, as becomes painfully clear when you're hanging out with 85 percent work friends, a friend established during school—one with whom you did a fair amount of "coming of age"—is often worth about five acquaintances formed in adulthood. Because this old friend knew you when you were far more irresponsible and prone to doing things like taking mushrooms and running around naked on a school football field, you've established a level of trust and honesty that is almost impossible to re-create with people who have only known you in the context of "adulthood." To your grown-up friends, you are a responsible human being with good prospects for the future and serious opinions about offshore drilling. To your old friends, though, you are the person who once ate fifteen Taco Bell soft tacos without vomiting to win $30.

It should also be stated that, despite old friends' clear benefits, there is serious danger in becoming "that guy" who only remains friends with the people he knew from school and never actually branches out to explore other social options in life. If you've ever borne witness to a social group collapse in on itself from constant, undiluted exposure to the same people well into adulthood, you know that it is a path littered with semi-insanity and a fear of the unknown that can cripple even the most well-adjusted person.

Family Friends

As you become more of a whole, rational human being with the ability to see things for what they are, you may start to realize that your family is not just one homogenous, terrible mass out to stop you from living your ideal life. Everyone from your parents to your cousins to your drunk aunts can become potential friends in adult life, people with whom you can relate and communicate in a way that is at once intensely familiar and relatively light. Few things are more satisfying than being able to go out drinking with family members once deemed tragically uncool and realizing that they are, indeed, awesome. There is also the added bonus of being able to confide in them in a way that you cannot with anyone else, as they are linked to you by blood and have watched you grow literally since birth.

It should be said, though, that the distinction between friend and family—though capable of being blurred from time to time—should never be eroded completely. Aside from the obvious catastrophes created by parents who want, even at a young age, to be "cool friends" with their children instead of the crucial authority figures they need to be, a fight between any two family members that would otherwise be manageable between actual friends can result in battles of cataclysmic passive-aggressiveness that no one should have to endure. Family friends are wonderful, but these friendships must be treated with caution.

Going-Out Friends

While they may come from all over your various social engagements and daily activities, going-out friends are, by definition, just that—the people you do most of your partying with. They are friends who seem to exist only in the context of drinking and/or staying out really late, and don't serve a much deeper purpose in terms of sharing ideas, secrets, or opinions about the world around you. Unlike work friends, you are not required to see them every day and accept the shame that comes with acting like a humongous mess in front of everyone at the bar last night. And unlike your old friends, they do not come with an entire subway car full of baggage from your shared history together. They are simply people with whom you can let your hair down and have a good time. Though, as we all likely know, it is often far too easy to get sucked into the trap of seeing too much of your going-out friends—a group that often includes people who are tap-dancing along the borderline of a serious substance abuse problem—and this can end in an imbalanced life full of unfulfilling sex and coke. It is best to keep them on the periphery of your social life, where they can do the least harm and provide the most benign amusement.

The key, it would seem, is branching out as much as possible and starting friendships with people you wouldn't normally run into in your daily life. And while making the effort to actually get to know people, such as your cooler-than-average barista or the friend of a friend who always brings a nice bottle of something to house parties and has good facial hair, can be intimidating, it brings with it a vastly expanded network of people to call friends. I think we've all seen what can happen to people who don't take

ADULT FRIENDS VS. KID FRIENDS

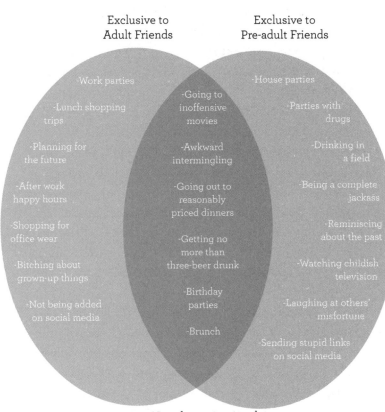

Exclusive to
Adult Friends

Exclusive to
Pre-adult Friends

-Work parties

-Lunch shopping
trips

-Planning for
the future

-After work
happy hours

-Shopping for
office wear

-Bitching about
grown-up things

-Not being added
on social media

-Going to
inoffensive
movies

-Awkward
intermingling

-Going out to
reasonably
priced dinners

-Getting no
more than
three-beer drunk

-Birthday
parties

-Brunch

-House parties

-Parties with
drugs

-Drinking in
a field

-Being a complete
jackass

-Reminiscing
about the past

-Watching childish
television

-Laughing at others'
misfortune

-Sending stupid links
on social media

Non-denominational

the time to expand their horizons when it comes to friends as they get further and further into adulthood, and they generally seem to retreat into their children, through whom they live vicariously, and convince themselves that having something resembling an active social life is a luxury that they simply cannot afford. As someone whose parents have always put a high premium on developing a diverse circle of friends and were curious when it comes to finding new people to hang out with, I remain convinced that collapsing in on yourself is not the only option.

Hell, even the Internet is a rich source of finding platonic soul mates from around the world. I have been told on more than one occasion that the friends I have acquired and maintain online—and not only the ones I haven't yet encountered IRL—are somehow not "real" friends. I stand firmly in the opposite camp, however, and have tangible proof in my many solid connections with people whom I simply started talking to regularly because their blog was hilarious and/or incredibly intelligent. Better still, this option doesn't even require getting dressed and leaving the house (always a plus in my book). With the advent of the Internet, you have no excuse not to find people who share your interests at every turn, and continually expand your options when it comes to doing things together.

The idea that friendship is something that stagnates in adulthood is easy to understand. People are less open to starting new things, much more consumed with their professional and romantic lives, and less certain about what it means to "hang out" with someone when it is no longer acceptable to constantly binge-drink at every social occasion. The truth is that making friends is more difficult when you are a grown-up, because with every day we get older, we get more rigidly set in these social lanes that the world around us seems convinced we should never abandon.

But the world is also full of potentially awesome people who love all the same weird movies and erotic fan fiction that you do, and there is no reason to deny yourself the pleasure of their company just because you think adults aren't supposed to meet new people if they're not trying to bone them. Falling in love with a new boyfriend or girlfriend can be thrilling, but so can falling for a new best friend.

Chapter 8

GROWING UP

Or, Making the World
a Better Place
by Doing Something
Other Than
Suckling from
Society's Ravaged Teat

esponsibility is a strange, ugly word. It conjures up in even the most balanced, rational person horrifying images of being expected to do things, day in and day out, that are both un-fun and provide little personal reward. It means taking the high road when you want to take the lowest emotional road possible; it means making decisions that come at great personal cost to you and may not be immediately beneficial; it means admitting you are wrong when all you want to do is plug your ears and scream about how you're a princess and princesses never apologize. When we pictured adulthood, it was usually some endless rainbow-hued mosaic of getting to choose your own bedtime, eating cake for dinner whenever you felt like it, and having sleepovers at any and all times (and we didn't even picture the sex that went along with this imagined stage of life!). "Responsibility" was always the gray, sad-faced cloud that hung over everything we were going to do with an audible "womp, womp" and occasional downpours of unexpected bills.

And yet every day, seemingly without warning, we take on more and more of this responsibility. We become indebted to those around us—both metaphorically and, in the case of cruel, terrifying banks, literally—and shoulder more burdens than just our own. We have significant others we have to take into consideration, family who expect to be given presents in return at Christmas (I know!?! What?!?), and friends we have to make more than a little effort to go and visit at regular intervals. It's as though a life of full-on adulthood and maturity sort of constructs itself around you, while you're still in the heady throes of "Oh, my God, I can drink whenever I want and eat however many tubes of Pringles my body will allow!" It's something that we don't choose—it chooses us. (You can have that one for free, motivational poster companies.)

If we ever needed a perfect example of expectation as opposed to brutal, brutal reality when it comes to entering the once rosy-seeming era of being a grown-up, consider the whole mess of student loans. There we were, idealistic and fresh-faced, ready to get all this book learnin' so we could be well on our way to a nondescript job that fulfills all our emotional and financial needs while reaffirming that we belong to an educated, superior class of society because we made the temporary yet crucial investment in a college degree. And then there was the whole part after the fact, after all that Pell Grant money got siphoned off into bottles of Rikaloff and Mad Dog, when no one gives a fuck about anything you did unless it was engineering or computer science, and you're basically just going to have to work at a restaurant and live with your parents for a while, and put an egregious amount of your weekly earnings toward repaying a debt that you refuse to even acknowledge the full extent of.

Our lives in the real world have started off with about as cold a bitch slap as one could possibly ask for—in the financial department, no less, where we are least equipped to deal with it—and yet debt is but a drop in the bucket against an ocean of all the things we have to learn. Regardless of whether we want to catch up to those around us and build something out of our Credit Cards Gone Crazy lives, we're going to have to eventually fashion ourselves into something resembling a coherent, responsible adult.

What do we think of, though, when we think of an adult? Surely we don't think of ourselves. We more likely think of our parents, or authority figures from childhood—people who were seemingly let in on a sacred guide to life that explains all of the more complex inner workings of the world around them. When you scraped a knee, or had a question about math class, or had your tiny little heart broken in a playground dispute, adults were there with the kind of sage advice that would seem like gospel to your naive eyes. Adults were almost a separate species, something that you could certainly never become—at least not if you didn't take this magical night class that they all seemed to attend, which taught them all the tricks and shortcuts to living life knowledgeably. (We're excluding the more drunken-or-cat-covered aunts and uncles in our lives whom we knew, from a very young age, were not quite in the grown-up column. For argument's sake, let's pretend they don't exist.)

The real surprise, of course, comes when you find out that none of this navigating-daily-life-with-a- bit-of-panache-and-intelligence shit comes with SparkNotes. While we were all convinced that there was some mystical hallway you passed through between school and real life, where a series of benevolent wizards were going to come teach you how to balance your checkbook and mow the lawn at regular intervals, it turns out that you basically just stop going to school at a certain point and then it's like "'K, cool, now get a job, human sloth. It's time for you to start contributing to society." (And no matter how much ugly crying you do, The Man isn't going to suddenly absolve your debt and give you a sweet apartment to live in rent-free. I tried.)

The bottom-line idea here is that you're basically going to have to figure everything out by yourself, no matter how much they tried to convince us that that one Home Ec class in seventh grade was going to make domestic life a worry-free dance in a mint julep fountain. So much of what constitutes "being a responsible person" is just stuff you discover as you go along, usually by making terrible, expensive, heartbreaking mistakes and falling flat on your face in front of important people. The only way you're going to know not to date the gorgeous, condescending cheater with the chest tattoo is to date him and have your soul urinated on by his callousness. The only way you're going to understand how important maintaining a good budget is is to find yourself at the crossroads of "Everything is expensive" and "Oh, fuck, I have no money." The only way you're going to stop getting fucked over on apartments is by having it happen one time and realizing that you probably shouldn't sublet from a cokehead you found on Craigslist who insists on being paid in $100 bills.

And let's not even pretend that we're in the ballpark of officially considering ourselves fully grown. Yes, technically we can sign contracts and we're expected to pay bills and not make verbal agreements for important financial decisions, but we are still very much amateurs. We are legally adults, but much more in the "underpaid assistant" phase of the ordeal than the "respected upper management" stage. There are going to be achievements and goalposts and obstacles that mark the road toward being a fully functioning grown-up, and we have passed only a few of them. Of course, this doesn't mean that we can throw up our hands and be like, "Welp, fuck it, I'm just going to treat people like shit when it suits me and drain my checking account on a regular basis because I'm young and beautiful and immortal." It just means that the stumblings and hesitant false starts are to be expected.

We'll all occasionally joke about how "Oh, God, I'm so old" when you see a group of fourteen-year-olds standing in front of the movie theater sharing one stolen cigarette among ten people and making out with each other wearing what appear to be JNCO jeans—but we know that we're not really old. In fact, the only reason we can even say things like that and get the kind of hesitant laugh we do is because we know that we sound like enormous, self-absorbed dickheads when we go off about how world-weary we are at the ripe old age of twenty-five. If anything, we're terrified at how young we are in comparison to a world that seems very much grown-up and not accommodating to people who are having a hard time figuring things out and/or making ends meet. We'll joke about our stodginess, but we know that we're still collectively getting our bearings.

Which is perhaps why it's so disorienting when we see people around us doing things like getting married, moving away, having children, or making decisions with someone other than themselves at the forefront of their minds. Sure, it's easy to mock the first parent among you and point out all the hilarious, semi-irritating-for-those-around-them things that come with having a kid, but at least some of that mockery stems from a twitchy kind of nervousness. Every time our friends and loved ones get older, every time they take a conscious step forward toward an invisible goalpost marked *maturity*, we wonder if we are falling too far behind. No one lives in a vacuum, and to pretend that the growth of those around us isn't a little terrifying would be disingenuous. We are all constantly making small increments of progress, but there are undeniably big social and personal markers that draw a clear line in the sand through your life. It may be funny to tease the first parent, but what about the last? Will the person who takes the longest to jump these life hurdles (if she does so at all) become the subject of mockery or, worse, pity?

We are happy for our friends and their achievements, of course. We want them to find the spouse of their dreams, or move to the country that suits them best, or do whatever they want in life, no matter how far away from us, geographically and emotionally, it may take them. But there is going to be a part of us that says, "No, wait, come back," even if we don't vocalize it. And it's not just asking for them to stay the same, it's asking yourself. It's imploring everything around you and within you to remain safe, and familiar, and young, and free of the real cares of life, which start to look scarier and more difficult as we get older. As long as no one is making these big changes, or declaring that he is becoming a new person with new goals and priorities, nothing needs to be called into question. If the gang is still together and going to the same happy hour, what is there to fear? It is only when someone breaks off or reminds you that his life is continuing to evolve, even if yours is not, that we are forced to confront just how much comfort we find in stability.

Recently, a friend my age was having a child, and, beyond the initial feelings of "Oh, my God, that's so awesome and weird!," there were a million and one questions about what this meant for every life it touched. Was she ready? What does it mean to be "ready"? Would I be ready to do the same thing if the opportunity presented itself? How much of my wanting to have a child is based on society's insistence that it is my feminine destiny to have one, and how much of it is genuine? Will this make her into a different person? Is that a bad thing? What will this child be like? What will all our children be like, and the generation they belong to? Of course it's selfish to ask all these questions about yourself upon hearing news that is undeniably centered in someone else's life, but it is also human. There are people who say that they are totally unaffected by the choices their friends make and the lifestyles they live, but those people are full of shit. We are all susceptible to peer pressure and comparison, even if it's ugly to admit. I'll be real here, though: Few things have inspired in me greater existential terror than seeing the inside of my friend's uterus pop up nonchalantly on my news feed.

These signifiers of serious development, aside from indicating that we're each taking meaningful steps in the direction of the life we want to be living, are clear reminders of how different the twenties can look on different people. Some people are getting married at twenty-two and settling down in a moderately priced condo they love decorating and posting photos of on Facebook. Some people are having a hard time holding down a job for more than three weeks at a time that doesn't involve following soap bubble artists around music festivals and being paid in burritos with doses of acid in them. Some people are staying in the city they grew up in and doing a whole lot of the same things you remember them doing in high school. And none of these are better or worse than the other (even if music festival guy may regret not building any kind of skill set/nest egg when he begins to lose his hair), but you are going to be surrounded by all of them.

In fact, simply by being in constant proximity to people who, despite their same age bracket, live lives nothing like one another, you may start to gain a little more perspective on what it is that you want to be doing. Even if you are, say, putting in forty hours a week in an office job you're perfectly content with, there is a good chance that you are going to be friends with—at least in the online sense—people who are eschewing that lifestyle completely. They may be taking a road trip across the country and performing their music in dive bars, or setting up a booth at renaissance fairs and selling all the beaded jewelry that is not quite twee enough to make it onto Etsy. And in looking at these images, at the people who are doing things with their life and their youth that you never really considered a possibility, you may feel a snide sense of superiority or you may feel envious. You may feel as though whatever you're doing isn't good enough, or isn't fun enough. And they very well may look at you and see the picture of "true adult" that they have never really been able to capture themselves.

The trick is not to imagine that this is some kind of awards ceremony at the end of an Olympic event, where everyone is being put on pedestals according to how well they are performing and ranked in direct competition with one another. While it's true that certain quantifiable factors go into "where everyone is," such as salary, there is no magical rule of the universe stating that for each additional dollar someone earns in comparison to you, she is going to be that much happier. There are plenty of arbitrary ways that we could categorize one another and attempt to quantify our exact level of personal fulfillment, but the truth is, we'll never really know. The second you stop looking around at everyone growing up in positive ways and thinking about how pathetic and stunted your own personal progress is, that's the second you can start really enjoying things. Of course, this is much easier said than done.

It's arguably more difficult now than it has ever been to simply let go of the comparisons with your peers while simultaneously remaining happy for what they are doing. Every day, whether we want to or not, we are bombarded with images and updates and self-congratulatory posts about all the wonderful things that are happening for them. (Or constant, minute-by-minute break-downs of what unemployed people are thinking about/listening to while they chill out on social media all day.) Everywhere we look, we find a new update on what is happening in the life of someone we're not even sure we want to know, a person with whom we've long since lost the ability to relate to, but who still fills our online life with bursts of "Look what I'm doing!" There is a sort of grotesque desire to look-while-not-seeing, to absorb every last bit of this information without ever feeling as if you're prying. (No one wants to feel as if they're too heavily invested in the goings-on of their extended group of acquaintances.)

But we are prying. And we want people to do it. It is the reason we most often take to our various platforms every time some-thing good happens to us; we want to confirm that it happened, and hear how proud of us everyone is, and bask in the joy for as long as is socially acceptable. We are all constantly marinating in this tepid stew of everyone else's humblebragging, of the more gratuitous moments we allow ourselves to announce what awesome things have been happening in our lives. No matter how much we don't want to engage too deeply, no matter how often we feel that we are too well-informed about everyone else just by browsing a few home pages, this is the environment we exist in. Escaping it—or at least rising above it—is about as complicated as it is futile. We'll always be able to find out about what is going on in everyone else's world. (Hell, your friends might even *call* you to tell you the good news.)

The most obvious places to start when looking for burgeoning adulthood and quantifiable maturity are clearly in arenas like the professional. We all need a job of some kind, and what exactly society has deemed you worthy of doing for monetary compensation is a pretty visible defining factor. We have a tendency, whether we actively do it or not, to place a higher social premium on jobs that pay better, are more difficult to land, generally take place in an office setting, and often require you to dress in a way that can only be described as "business casual." Yes, it is wrong to unilaterally say that these people are more "grown up" than someone who works in, say, a restaurant, but this is often the way people are going to judge you.

Or they might look at where you live. They will take a look at your apartment—where it's located, how much graffiti is on the subway station or bus stop nearest your house, how much of the furniture came from a garage sale—and make assumptions about who you are as a person. They might feel envious of your decorating skills, or curious as to how you got a place in such a prime yet not incredibly noisy location, or smugly superior about living in a place they deem so much better, depending on the kind of place you're staying in. There will even be people who are big enough delusional douchebags to think that your zip code defines you, that it puts some invisible checkmark next to the word *cool* floating above your head.

And there is always who you are dating, a signifier of achievement unmatched by nearly anything else, especially among women. Whether we like it or not, we are told since we are old enough to idolize a Disney princess that a huge amount of our worth is going to be wrapped up in whether or not some investment banker with good taste in blazers rides up on a white horse covered in money and compliments and sweeps us off our feet. We are bombarded by messages every day—from the magazine covers we pass in the grocery store to our own concerned family members—who want to know if we're dating someone and, if so, how well it is going. For many people, dating in the twenties becomes nothing short of some bizarre Japanese game show that leads up to marriage. It's just a series of hilarious trials and tribulations that, unless ending in universal approval and a sizable diamond, will be considered by some to be worthless. Some people are going to openly judge you based on what your dating status is, and it's hard to avoid them on sight alone. For nearly every life choice you make as an adult, you'll encounter someone passive-aggressively telling you that it isn't good enough.

Perhaps one of the best antidotes in your own life, though, is to start actively trying to think about people (and the level of "adulthood" you would give them on some imaginary scale) in terms of emotional maturity. While certain people well into middle age and beyond have the emotional development of a petulant child, and seem to fly through life with complete disregard to things as insignificant and cumbersome as "other people's feelings," that is no reason not to aspire to greater things ourselves. Undoubtedly, you'll find people in your group of friends, in your family, in your inner circle, whom you would consider to be "better people" than most. They listen, they keep their promises, they know how to apologize, and they are generally respectful of other people's humanity. No matter what these people are doing in their lives professionally, or how far along they are on their journey to purchasing a two-bedroom apartment in a desirable part of the city, they have something to actually be proud of about their progress as a human being.

And the patience we have for people who are not interested in being thoughtful or respectful diminishes—or at least should diminish—as we age. To be perfectly frank, at a certain point, it just gets fucking exhausting to hang out with people who aren't stepping their game up at least slightly when it comes to how they treat those around them. There is only so much we can associate with people who are jealous, or irresponsible, or judgmental, or angry, before we start becoming those things ourselves. And it's undeniable that friendships with people whom you can trust implicitly, who you know like you for who you are and not some janky notion of social obligation, are way more enjoyable to have around. It's just nice knowing that you can relax and be yourself around people, and the people who exude this kind of "I'm not an uptight asshole" vibe tend to attract better people.

Why isn't there more of an emphasis placed on how we're evolving when we interact with one another? With the difficulty everyone is having in finding the professional success we once naively hoped to be entirely defined by, you would hope that breaking up with someone in a more intelligent, caring manner at twenty-five than you did at fifteen would be a milestone that is much appreciated, if not rewarded with financial compensation. No one is saying that we need to go from cripplingly petty to a sexier combination of Gandhi and John Lennon overnight, but if we're not aiming for self-improvement, what are we doing? There are few things more frustrating than seeing people who, despite any leaps they may be making in the rest of their lives, are still living out the same patterns emotionally that they've been in since adolescence. It is worse, of course, when we are doing it ourselves.

I often catch myself, as I imagine many of us do, in a moment of emotional immaturity that reminds me of just how much growing lies ahead of me. I'll be having an argument with someone and I'll be quick to speak before I think about how much shit what I'm saying will get me into, or I'll say something hurtful just because I feel wronged myself and want to get a cheap shot in to feel as if I'm getting even. It's stupid, and I know it is, but sometimes I can't help it. And then I'll have a hard time mustering up a legitimate apology because I still have a massive chip on one of my shoulders that is constantly whispering into my ear, "You don't need to say sorry to this bitch, you are flawless, don't even worry about it." No matter how much I'm achieving in any other aspect of my life, knowing that I'm still capable of treating people like an impatient, selfish child when it suits me reminds me that, in many ways, I am still very much using the training wheels on my independence.

But to recognize these moments, to say to myself, *Hey, this is shitty, and I should stop being such a shitty person right now,* is already a more adult move than I was ever prepared to make in the past. I look back on eighteen-year-old Chelsea—whose life was pretty much a series of shenanigans and hijinks in which I inserted my foot ever more violently into my mouth and dated guys who enjoyed treating me like something recently scraped off the bottom of their shoe—and feel secure in the knowledge that I am treating everyone better now, including myself. No matter how criminally underrated it may be, this respectful and thoughtful treatment of yourself is perhaps the first real step to making constructive emotional choices. You're never going to wake up magically one day and think, *I'm gonna stop hanging out with people who make me feel like a leper and maybe start building constructive friendships with people who are kind to me* unless you believe that you're the kind of person who deserves it.

At the risk of sounding like a wall hanging your grandmother needlepointed for you, feeling that you deserve it is probably the biggest component of all this. Because there is only so much success you're going to achieve in any area of your life if you don't think you're a good person who is worthy or capable of any of the things you're doing. (Except maybe in the professional arena, since I've met several people who work in finance whom I could only describe as dead behind the eyes, but they make a fuck-ton of money, so good for them.) For most of us normals, however, feeling sincerely as though we are cool, interesting, good people we would want to hang out with if given the choice is a pretty essential component of growing up, it would seem.

We've all met people who ooze confidence, and not in that dicky way that gives the distinct impression that they like the smell of their own farts more than anyone should. These people just seem genuinely happy with themselves, even if they wear clothes that other people consider goofy-looking or aren't super-attractive or don't make a ton of money. They are generally cool to be around because their confidence and self-assuredness is a kind of port in a never-ending storm of "Is what I'm doing okay??? Do you like this???" that we're bombarded with from the vast majority of our friends and social media. It has a tendency to rub off on people when you're just incredibly happy with yourself and don't really need anyone's approval. (Ironically enough, it tends to be the people who aren't terribly caught up in what others think of them who end up getting the most respect and admiration.)

The truth is, that no matter how much you feel as if you and only you are a giant fuckup and everyone else around you is laughing and dancing as romantic success and hundred-dollar bills rain down on them, everyone is confused. I don't know a single person in my life—no matter how successful in any given aspect of her life—who feels as though she's got everything on lock and is now putting life on autopilot and coasting through until she reaches a perfectly contented death somewhere in old age. And even the people who have somehow mastered several important things in life all at once and find themselves with relatively few logistical problems are then presented with the existential meltdown that is "Am I becoming boring?" In a way, the thrill of being unsure about things is so much of what we love; it's hard not to get at least a little contact high out of feeling like everything ahead of you is open and unknown.

Speaking personally, I was never a confident person growing up. It usually happens that way when you're awkward-looking with braces and cystic acne and a weird sense of humor and glasses in a shape so unflattering that selling them to unsuspecting young tweens should be a crime—you're not terribly well-liked. You don't get to feel enormously good about yourself. It's hard, especially for people who grow up feeling that they're unpopular or that they don't have a distinct place in life, to ease into an adulthood where they genuinely feel that they're carving out the life they want to be living.

For me, and I'm sure for many others, choosing to see the good parts of yourself and think more about what you're doing well and what is within your control to change rather than languishing over how tragically uncool or unsuccessful you are is not an easy thing to do. It's so much more natural to pick on yourself, to see all the things you are not measuring up in, to watch your friends doing things with their lives you are terribly envious of or scared by and wonder why your life is not moving in a similar direction.

But at a certain point, constantly picking on yourself and thinking about how you are not good enough is just exhausting. I could spend all day browsing through Facebook and counting the times I see someone I miss who doesn't care about me, or someone whose life I wish I had. I could do what I have almost always done, which is think about what part of me isn't pretty or smart or growing up quickly enough. I could think about where everyone is, as if we're all running some kind of hundred-yard dash and place myself directly in front of or behind people, depending on how much money we make or whom we're dating. And I've done that; I think we all have. We're not getting grades anymore. We're not all living together. We're not hanging out in the same social circles—we have to have some rubric to measure ourselves against.

I have tried, though, in the past year or so, to remind myself of the things I do well in life, of what I can be proud of, even if someone else doesn't think it's impressive enough. I make lists of the things I don't like in my life, things that I can change, and I work on them. I try to pay bills as efficiently as I can, and work hard, and be comfortable in what I've achieved at the end of each day. And I try, most of all, to be a little easier on myself. I will never be as pretty or as rich or as well-liked as someone else, and there is nothing wrong with that. As much as these messages of self-love have become cloying platitudes, there really is nothing truer. Being kind and patient with yourself is a choice you can make every day, and when you make it, you realize that every other aspect of your life—from getting that promotion to meeting the kind of people you want to surround yourself with—becomes, as if by magic, just that much easier.

Maybe that is what makes you an adult more than anything else in your life. To look at what you're doing and honestly say, "I am trying my hardest and being kind to people, and I like who I am" is something that so many people—regardless of where society might place them on any number of scales—cannot say about themselves. You can list a million reasons not to feel like a grown-up yet, to feel like you have so far to go and so much to prove to everyone before you can kick back and feel like the master of any kind of domain. But to make the choice every day to take responsibility for what you can change, to decide that you are not going to bullshit your way through with whiny diatribes about how it's everyone else's fault and never your own (which I must cop to having done for an extended period of time), or how you are never going to be as good as this or that person so why even try, seems like a pretty good place to start.

You could always be doing something better, and there will always be someone you're slightly envious of. And until you reach whatever imagined plateau of "My life is awesome and perfect and impervious to criticism," you're just going to have to deal with that. (Spoiler alert: You're probably going to die before you ever reach that plateau.) If you can do one favor for yourself, and put one checkmark in the "mature" column for yourself, let it be realizing that just because one friend has a better job, or another one is getting married, or your ex has moved on before you, you are not a worthless child who doesn't deserve the lofty title of "young adult." You're just figuring it out with the rest of us, and this isn't some county fair contest called Who Can Construct a Nuclear Family in under Five Years Out of College. It's called Life, and you are going to be playing it for the next several decades at least, so you might want to pace yourself on the "I am an unequivocal failure who doesn't deserve to take up space in this coffee shop" front. I promise you're doing much better than you think.

ACKNOWLEDGMENTS

I would like to thank my family for always supporting me in my imperfect journey. (Especially Mama Bear, who protects her cubs with the razor-sharp claws of love.) Anthony, I am Rocky and you are cutting my eyes in the corner of the ring so I can keep fighting. Jordana, I am a better writer because of you (and your infinite patience). To Chris, thank you for giving me my first home as a writer—the best team I could hope for—and for believing in my work. Finally, I owe you everything, Marc. I could not have written this book without you, and I will always be trying to be as good a human as you are. Thank you, everyone.